Cranked Up Really High

Genre Theory and Punk Rock

STEWART HOME

CODEX

1995

First published July 1995
New edition February 1996

CodeX
P.O. Box 148
Hove
BN3 3DQ
UK

British Library Cataloguing in Publication
Data. A catalogue record for this book is
available from the British Library.

ISBN 1899598 01 4

Printed in England by Page Bros (Norwich)

Stewart Home was born in South London in 1962. His activities and fields of interest have long defied categorisation. In addition to his role as prime propagandist for the Neoist Cultural Conspiracy, he is a novelist, musician, performance artist, more recently an occultist, and according to several sources 'an egomaniac on a world historical scale'. Stewart Home is single and lives in London where he spends his time pursuing an interest in Hegelian philosophy and composing satirical magazine articles about the royal family.

Contents

They (journalists) always ask stupid questions like 'What does mummy think?' you know. They ask 'What's behind it?' Stupid. There's nothing significant or shocking about what we do. We just play for ourselves, to kids like ourselves. There's nothing behind it.

Ian Woodcock of Eater.

We're not pretending to be dole queue members. We're middle class and we go to school. I can't be a punk when I'm forty, so I'm learning to play tenor sax. Then I can go off and play at Butlin's when I'm past it.

Jeremy Valentine of the Cortinas.

We don't want to get into a big intellectual thing. We just want to play rock 'n' roll. Just being original is showing intelligence.

Johnny Ramone of the Ramones.

INTRODUCTION
TO THE SECOND ENGLISH EDITION

In the eighteen months since *Cranked Up Really High* was first published I've had plenty of feedback, both good and bad. However, it seems that a lot of those reviewing the book misunderstood my thesis, since it was often described as an 'I was there account of punk rock'. As anyone who bothers to read the book can see, I am actually disputing the contention that there was any 'centre' to the punk rock 'phenomena' to be 'at'. The cover strapline on the first edition declaring the work to be 'an inside account of punk rock', used the term 'inside' in a phenomenological rather than common sense fashion. The confusion many reviewers exhibited about this can only be attributed to stupidity. I was not responsible for the title of the Italian translation *Marci, sprochi e imbecilli 1976-1996: la rivolta punk non si è mai fermata* (Castelvecchi, Rome 1996), which was genuinely misleading.

Much to my delight, *Cranked Up Really High* succeeded in getting up the noses of anally-retentive record collector scum, who now have to suffer my scorn alongside that of various individuals responsible for bootlegging ultra-rare super-dumb sleaze-bag thud from the late seventies and early eighties. That's punk for you punk, if you ain't up for slagging the things you dig most, then you just don't have the necessary ATTITUDE! 'Scuse me while I pour myself a shot of McClelland's finest Single Malt Islay Scotch Whisky. That's better! Anyway, while record collector scum fail to understand that the point of accumulating info is to marshal it into an argument, they have their uses as trivia merchants who can be consulted by those who know that facts alone are useless things. There is a huge difference between playing DUMB and being genuinely STOOPID. This explains why I rate the Queers and loathe lumpen-intellectuals Britpop wannabes.

Strangely, not a single reviewer picked up on the fact that throughout the book I parody various styles of rock 'journalism'. Instead, I was offered advice along the lines of 'Masterswitch didn't disappear completely, they changed their name to Jimmy Edwards and the Profile and later evolved into Time UK with Rick Butler from the Jam'. As though I give a flying fuck about a bunch of non-league losers. Moving from junk to punk, classic seventies platters keep making it onto CD, two of the best recent releases being the

Short Sharp Shock: Independent Recordings UK 1977 compilation and *Outrage & Horror* by the Art Attacks. I did the excellent band interview in the booklet accompanying the latter CD and both releases are on Overground, parent company of Codex who published the book you're holding in your hands. Buy the product suckers, I want Overground to shower me with free CDs. Likewise, although the reference to McClelland's in the proceeding paragraph may strike some readers as gratuitous, it is called placement and I'm hoping the company will ship me a free crate of their finest Islay Whisky as a reciprocal gesture of friendship.

Stewart Home, London, December 1996

I
JOURNALIST JIVE
A critique of previous works on Punk Rock

The three quotes used as epigrams at the front of this text can all be found in the coffee-table picture book *Punk Rock* by Virginia Boston (Penguin New York/Plexus London 1978). In some ways it is tempting to simply print these quotes on a post card and mail them around the world with the additional information that this is all that needs to be said about Punk Rock. Unfortunately, the more that's written about a subject, the more there is to say about it. With the growth of cultural studies in recent years, a great deal of quasi-academic literature has been produced around the subject of Punk Rock. Commentaries generate further commentaries and secondary sources proliferate like flies around a fresh turd.

It has thus become necessary to demonstrate that Punk Rock is/was not 'profound', is/was not a 'manifestation of the avant-garde' and that anyone 'looking for the meaning of life in a plastic platter' is wasting their time. I am not arguing that Punk did/does not reflect the society that produced it; nor that, from the perspectives of cultural studies or sociology, it is pointless to pursue it as an object of study. Nor am I suggesting that those who participated in 'the movement' are able to fix its meaning once and for all. Indeed, as a musical genre I would suggest that rather than being stable and static, Punk Rock is fluid and its boundaries are subject to ongoing renegotiation. It is the failure of much quasi-academic writing on the subject to address these issues that invalidates them as works of criticism.

The most absurd book published to date on Punk Rock is *Break All Rules: Punk Rock And The Making Of A Style* by Tricia Henry (UMI Research Press, Ann Arbor 1989). This work appears to be adapted from a Ph.D. dissertation undertaken at New York University's Department of Performance Studies and can be most profitably (mis)read as a parody of academic research. One of the more ludicrous category errors made by Henry is to be found on page 134 of the book where she compares the Billboard chart placings of the songs *I'm A Believer* and *Heroin*. Since only the former song was released as a single it is hardly surprising that while it was a number one hit, the latter failed to gain a chart placing at all! It should go without saying that only songs released in a single format are eligible for a place in the Billboard singles chart, although Henry doesn't seem to know this.

Henry also appears ignorant of other books on the subject because she claims in the preface that 'a serious study of punk rock and the evolution of its style has not previously been undertaken' (page ix). The best academic text dealing with this subject is actually One Chord Wonders: Power And Meaning In Punk Rock by Dave Laing (Open University Press, Milton Keynes/Philadelphia 1985); this will be dealt with below. Fourteen of the sixteen research interviews conducted by Henry, and listed in the bibliography (pages 145-6) took place in 1986. Since the bulk of Henry's 'research' appears to have been conducted a year after Laing's book was published, it seems extraordinary that she should be ignorant of it.

Like other writers, Henry also suffers from an extremely simplistic notion of what constitutes both class and genre. On the latter, she sweepingly states that the Sex Pistols were the 'first and most notorious of the punk bands' (page 38). Later in this text I will outline the ways in which genre is socially negotiated, and shall argue against the notion of the Pistols being a 'PUNK' band at all, let alone the 'originators' of this genre. Here, it is enough to note that simply stating, as Henry does, that the Sex Pistols were the 'first' PUNK band, fails to establish the assertion as a fact.

Likewise, Henry takes the rhetoric about class made by various individuals associated with the PUNK ROCK 'movement' at face value, and as completely unproblematic. Thus she baldly claims that 'punk in Britain was essentially a movement consisting of underprivileged working class white youths' (page 67). Again, rather than being stable and static, class is actually a fluid category and the rhetorical use made of this notion by various individuals associated with PUNK can most accurately be described as a form of theatre. I will deal with this below.

As someone who insists on viewing pop music through the prism of the avant-garde, Henry consistently misapplies categories to her material. For example, she claims that transvestism was taken up by glam rockers who were 'preoccupied with subject matter and behaviour that shocked the middle classes' (page 34). This harping on 'épater les bourgeoisie' misses the point because transvestism is as likely to shock blue collar workers as their white collar bosses. Being more firmly rooted in generational than in class differences, rock usually sets out to shock parents in general, and not simply individuals who view themselves as belonging to the middle or upper classes.

Since I'm more interested in PUNK records than erroneous commentaries upon them, I'll skip going over books by the likes of Greil Marcus and Clinton Heylin. In any case, I've reviewed these tomes in magazines such as *Variant* and *Here & Now*, so it's pointless exposing their flaws yet again when anybody interested in what I have to say about the subject can read my opinions elsewhere. Unfortunately, Marcus in particular has had an influence on other writers, one example being Neil Nehring author of *Flowers In The Dustbin: Culture, Anarchy And Postwar England* (University of Michigan Press 1993). It is not worth dealing with this absurd book in any depth and I will confine myself to citing a single example of it's author's inability to differentiate historical fact from the shameless fictions perpetrated in secondary texts. Nehring states on page 276:

> The SI [Situationist International] reached its apogee in the May Revolution of 1968, when it's slogans prominently decorated the walls of Paris. George Woodcock in his history of anarchism, cites in particular the slogan 'Imagination is seizing power!'

Of course, 'Power to the Imagination' (there are slight variations in the graffiti and how it was translated, but we can ignore these minor differences in wording) was a battle cry of the March 22nd Movement, and has no bearing on the subject under discussion. In fact, not only is this not a Situationist slogan, the SI criticised the formulation in an unattributed article entitled *The Beginning Of An Era* (*Internationale Situationiste 12*, English translation from *Situationist International Anthology* edited by Ken Knabb, Berkeley 1981):

> The movement was... a rejection of art that did not yet know itself as the historical negation of art (a rejection expressed in the poor abstract slogan 'Power to the Imagination' which did not know the means to put this power into practice, to reinvent everything, and which, lacking power, lacked imagination).

It is on the basis of erroneous historical exegesis of this type, which anyone who bothers to read the source material can see is absurd, that a number of hacks have fallaciously claimed that the Situationists were a major influence on the events of May '68, and the PUNK ROCK phenomenon. Indeed, the process of 'historification' is in reality one of 'simplification', where a great diversity of facts

11

are brought under a few clear, simple and hopelessly misleading headings. Thus many of the wilder aspects of sixties and seventies 'counter-culture' have been wrenched out of context and labelled as Situationist when they actually have nothing to do with the term.

Of more interest than the journalist jive churned out by Marcus and his imitators, is Dave Laing's *One Chord Wonders: Power And Meaning In Punk Rock.* In his introduction, Laing states that 'unlike nearly every other youth subculture (the Teds, Mods, Skinheads etc), punk began as music and punks themselves began as music fans and performers.' This is worth pursuing, because if PUNK is principally a musical genre we can concentrate on records and concerts.

Laing describes the music he views as having preceded and influenced PUNK – bands like the Who, MC5, New York Dolls and Stooges – as 'heavily rhythmic and richly chorded, guitar based with assertive vocals presented... with a white rock intonation, generally eschewing the mannerisms of soul singing.' By and large, this could also be taken as a description of PUNK. However, in PUNK, the singing lacks variety, it is straight rather than embellished. Despite a verse/chorus format, PUNK songs appear formless because heavy distortion is used on the guitar, so that the chords bleed into one another. Likewise, while the drums are syncopated, the bass is not, a break with previous pop traditions. Thus, depending upon which part of the rhythm section the listener concentrates on, a PUNK song may appear as forward driven or having reached a point of stasis.

However, Laing does not understand the lyrical content of PUNK (or indeed other forms of rock and pop music) which he tends to treat with a gravity that they do not deserve. Likewise, he has failed to grasp the fluid nature of PUNK as a musical genre and does not understand the forces that set it in motion or the direction in which it moves. Much of what Laing treats as PUNK simply doesn't cut it as such today, for example, the Stranglers (they have keyboards all over their records rather than being dominated by guitars, which Laing himself describes as defining the PUNK sound), or the Fall (art shit).

There are major problems with the table of lyric contents in Laing's book (page 27) which compares the first albums by the Damned, Clash, Stranglers, Sex Pistols and Vibrators to the Top 50 best selling singles in Britain in 1976. Most obviously problematic is the categorisation of *London Lady* by the Stranglers as belonging 'on the borderline between the "romantic" and "sexuality" categories, since the vocalist describes his "lady" in a highly objectified and hostile manner' (page 28). Clearly, Laing has difficulty in understanding rock lyrics (and as I've already observed, the Stranglers are not a PUNK band), because this song is actually a character assassination of the journalist Caroline Coon and should therefore be placed either in the novelty or personal feelings categories, it has nothing to do with romance.

Likewise, PUNK is assigned 0% novelty lyrics as opposed to 8% of the Top 50 records. Many of the PUNK lyrics attributed to other categories could equally well be understood as novelty items. Indeed, the genesis of PUNK itself is best understood as a dialectical interplay between the notions of novelty and genre which are projected further and further backwards as the world races into the future. Certainly, when I was fourteen years old and stumbled across the Sex Pistols in the autumn of 1976 on the *So It Goes* TV show, the group and their music appeared unprecedented to me. Two years later, when a seventeen year old told me that upon hearing *Anarchy In The UK* he thought it was going to cause a revolution, I could not refrain from laughing. Such literalism is ludicrous. Nevertheless, I must admit that at the close of 1976 I considered *Anarchy In The UK* and *Teenage Depression* by Eddie And The Hot Rods to be the best records ever made because, to my young ears (used to Chuck Berry, Geno Washington and T. Rex), they appeared to be the most novel songs ever recorded. However, this opinion was soon to change. Having begun reading the music press, I quickly became hip to the existence of Patti Smith, the MC5, Iggy And The Stooges, the New York Dolls, the Dictators, Richard Hell etc.

What I'm saying here is that our perceptions change over time. Thus, when I first heard *Anarchy In The UK*, on a TV show several months before it was released as a record, it appeared unprecedented, but within a year I realised that there were all sorts of precedents for it... Today – sod it, I'm gonna have to break my flow, get up and put the damn thing on my record player. The last time I can actually remember hearing the whole record in a single sitting was sometime last year in a pub called the Sugar Loaf, opposite the Masonic Grand Lodge in Holborn.

Problems, problems, I no longer have a seven inch copy of the *Anarchy In The UK* single and, in any case, I seem to remember there being two different mixes. Instead, I located my copy of *Never Mind The Bollocks* which includes the single. Listening to it again, it sounds a bit leaden and I'm left thinking how much I dislike Paul Cook's drumming, real meat and potatoes stuff, awful! Anyway, half way through the song the needle starts jumping all over the place, the platter is scratched.

Next, I pull out my copy of *Kiss This* plus bonus *Live In Trondheim* CD which I picked up for a fiver. The track sounds better on CD, tinnier, trashier. Has it been remixed or is this just the effect of two listenings in a row? I can't be bothered to work this out. Anyway, I still hate the drumming. Musically it comes across as an average to good rock record (the drumming really pulls it down); lyrically it still sounds like a novelty production (one great rhyme 'anarchist' with 'get pissed', which is almost as good as the Modern Lovers rhyming 'Picasso' and 'asshole'). Part of the problem seems to be that familiarity breeds contempt. More than anything else, *Anarchy In The UK* sounds like history.

The next thing I do is put on the Bollock Brothers version of the song. It sounds much better than the Sex Pistols, this is a full blooded novelty record! Johnny Rotten's voice is too expressive to work well on novelty or PUNK songs, he sounds like an artiste. Finally, I pull out a copy of *The Great Rock 'N' Roll Swindle* and play the Sex Pistols medley by the Black Arabs, which kicks off with a disco rendition of *Anarchy*. I like this even more than the Bollock Brothers. It still sounds fresh, partly because I've never been subjected to it in a pub. Whenever I've listened to the medley, it was after making a conscious decision to utilise it as a piece of entertainment.

What I'm establishing is that my perception of *Anarchy In The UK* and the Sex Pistols has changed over time. I'm not an essentialist. As far as I'm concerned, objects and ideas derive their meaning from their relationship to each other. There are no Platonic ideals or stable meanings. If PUNK, as the odd 'critic' has absurdly claimed, was a modern day version of Dada, I could conclude this discourse right now with the following observations: *Anarchy In The UK* was a novelty record; *Anarchy In The UK* was a PUNK record; therefore all novelty records are PUNK records. Unfortunately, the relationship between Dadaism, Situationism and PUNK is more elliptical than self-styled 'contemporary cultural critics' make out and so there remains much that needs to be said about it.

Part of the problem with PUNK is that as soon as strict definitions are applied to the subject, it begins to disappear. Common sense dictates that what we're dealing with is obvious, and yet, when we add the dimension of historical consciousness to our discussion, the subject eludes us. However, this problem isn't insurmountable, the differences between PUNK, new wave, hardcore etc, are socially negotiated. There is a good deal of agreement in the way specialist record shops categorise the goods they sell. What I've got to say here is based on the record shops I frequent, London branches of Record and Tape Exchange, Rhythm Records, Wreckless Records, Rough Trade, Select-A-Disk, Mr CD etc. For a start, there is a well established distinction between PUNK, hardcore and indie. Likewise, a distinction is sometimes made between PUNK and new wave, or seventies PUNK and later (which tends to be hardcore, or at least veering that way). Similarly, much of the output of groups who would have been considered 'PUNK' in 1977 (for example the Sex Pistols, Clash, Damned, Stranglers, Television, Blondie, Talking Heads, Boomtown Rats, Wire) has been assimilated into the rock and pop sections of specialist record shops, and can also be found in ordinary high street outlets. So again, we're seeing that PUNK as a musical genre is fluid, that it changes over time and that one of the ways in which it is socially negotiated is in the way record shops categorise the music they're selling. Of course, the social negotiation of a genre such as PUNK is also visible in the music press and specialist magazines such as *Record Collector*, in the interaction between musicians and their audiences, in the activities of record companies etc.

Before I began writing this text it seemed logical to take the position that, in fact, there was no such thing as a PUNK band, there were only PUNK records. However, since the subject is proving pretty elusive as it is, adopting such a rigorous approach would require too much hard work. After all, it is in itself fairly perverse to write thousands of words to prove that PUNK ROCK, something a few idiots (such as Groovy Greil Marcus) consider profound, is actually trivial. Partly my desire to make this point stems from an ingrained opposition to 'serious culture' and a wish to overthrow it. The decadence of high cultural discourse is revealed by the fact that its apologists feel the need to shore it up by appropriating PUNK ROCK and similar phenomena. Since the theorising of imbeciles such as Marcus is so inept, sabotaging his reactionary project does not require much effort. The fact that I am able to take 'intellectual' short cuts reflects my attitude to the subject under discussion, which as I have already said, is not of any great consequence. Of course, insisting that there were no PUNK bands, only PUNK records, would resolve the difficulty of how to treat the output of the Clash, but it would also create fresh problems. How, for example, do you deal with a band like Generation X, in many ways an archetypal PUNK band, who made pop rather than PUNK records?

Related to the changes in our perception of PUNK, are changes in consumer technology, most obviously in terms of the introduction of the Walkman and the CD. The Walkman put music right in my ears and enabled me to decipher lyrics that I'd been hearing for years without ever being able to work out what was being sung. Since I generally listen to my Walkman when I'm travelling on the underground, it's a waste of time playing spoken word cassettes or experimental music because of the background noise. As a consequence, this technology greatly increased the amount of PUNK ROCK that I heard. Again, PUNK is ideally suited to functions such as random play on CD, because track order is generally not of much consequence to the genre. Likewise, a great many PUNK songs that have been deleted for years are suddenly available again on CD.

Staying with the forces that shape PUNK as a genre, it's obvious that perception of a genre changes not only over time, but also according to the level of interest any given individual has in a particular area of music, or whatever. Thus, in recent years, there have been television advertised 'PUNK' compilation albums featuring groups such as the Jam, Stranglers, Members etc, whose individual records long ago moved out of the PUNK category and into the rock (or in the Jam's case perhaps the Mod) section of specialist record shops. In 1977, Phonogram was able to pass off its *New Wave* album (featuring the Ramones, Dead Boys, Patti Smith, New York Dolls, Runaways, Skyhooks, Richard Hell, Little Bob Story, Boomtown Rats, Talking Heads, Damned and Flamin' Grovies) as a PUNK platter. Such a record would not appeal to dedicated punk collectors today. The last punk compilation I bought (as opposed to blagged) was *Back To Front Volume 4* featuring Tits, Pekinska Patka, Standbys, Eat, Hurskas, P!I!G!Z!, Ignerents, M'n'M's, News, Fast Cars, Lightning Raiders, Johnny Concrete, Knots, Anorexia,

Widows, Rocks, City Kent, Tot Rocket And The Twins and Victimize. This CD was first issued in 1994, and the tracks it contains were recorded between 1978 and 1981. While I can recall seeing features in the British music press about everyone on the *New Wave* compilation, with the sole exception of the Skyhooks, and many of these acts achieved UK chart placings, I've never seen any coverage of the bands featured on *Back To Front Volume 4*. Indeed most of them have never had any product released in the UK. The tracks were originally issued in runs of a few hundred, selling to a very limited market in various parts of Europe, Australia and the United States, while the CD was compiled by Incognito Records of Germany.

What I'm beginning to expose is why the subject under discussion is so elusive; 'opposition' to the 'mainstream' is one of the things that defines PUNK to those engaged with the discourse. 'Real' PUNK tends to be invisible, because as soon as a group gains a mass audience, they cease being a PUNK band and become a rock or pop act. Of course, the idea that PUNK is 'underground', or at least 'oppositional', is problematic in terms of those post-modern theories that view our epoch as a time of proliferating margins. But then that part of the PUNK audience that has any interest in post-modernism is more than capable of resolving this 'contradiction' by adopting a pose of 'ironic' consumption. Besides, coherence is death, whereas living cultures are generated from the tensions generated around clusters of contradiction. With PUNK, one such cluster of tensions is formed around the twin poles of populism and elitism. While late seventies PUNK musicians, as 'dole queue rockers', indulge(d) in a great deal of rhetoric about accessibility and equality, many of the figures associated with the 'new wave' explosion were eager to join the jet-set rock elite, with their original fans being equally happy to abandon their 'heroes' to a mass audience, denouncing these 'idols' as sell-outs while simultaneously transferring their allegiance to less commercially successful bands.

There is a long tradition of snobbish individuals attempting to derive social status from the cult of obscurity, and the results are at times hilarious. Series of punk compilation albums such as *Killed By Death* or *Back To Front* appeal to the elitism of those who enjoy listening to records that their neighbours don't own. Of course, a lot of the music is damn fine but the fact that no one has heard of the bands enables those buying the records/CDs (or cassettes in the case of the *Hardcore History* series issued by Destroy Tapes of Hackney, London) to feel that they aren't part of the herd and are capable of searching out rare gems of culture. However, while I'd never heard of a good many of the bands featured on the *Back To Front* series before their music was issued on these compilations, the very first track on the first side of volume one was not only by a band that were familiar to me, I'd also seen them play live. The sleeve notes for *Idi Amin* by the K9's (1979, UK) are intended to reassure purchasers that this track is suitably obscure, thereby confirming their 'esoteric' tastes: 'this band is from England. They released only one 3 track EP, which was limited to 1000 copies.' I can imagine listeners who didn't attend late seventies PUNK gigs in south-east England thinking the K9's were seriously unknown, whereas I had a strange sense of deja vu. Not only had I seen the band supporting someone bigger, and possibly more than once, but at the time I hadn't thought much of them. Actually, I was pleasantly surprised by the song, which was much better than I remembered the band being live. Maybe it was just a bad gig or perhaps I wasn't in the right frame of mind.

However, it's not as though at least some of the people putting out and/or buying this stuff aren't consciously aware of these contradictions. Perhaps the best album of this type is the bootleg *Feel Lucky Punk?* which features the following sleeve notes:

> Greetings, Collector Scum! And welcome to the world of SNOTTY, OBNOXIOUS, 2-CHORD PUNK ROCK! This here album contains 22 fine examples o' straight-ahead, hard hitting, loud-fast-stupid '77-'78 rarities from AUSTRALIA, the USA and even 1 from a crew o' Swiss alpine yoddlers! No faggy speed-metal guitar virtuosos, no Dischordian 'awareness' – just plain ole violent, simple and sexist hate-mongering PUNK-ROCK, recorded while Henry Rollins was 'rocking' to Kansas.

Here, of course, we find another of the contradictions out of which PUNK ROCK is generated, the dialectical interplay between the 'authentic' and the 'counterfeit.' The problem with self-styled 'contemporary cultural critics' is that they are so concerned with the former that they inevitably expose themselves as the latter. Imagine actually liking the Au Pairs and the Gang Of Four! Groovy Greil Marcus doesn't seem to realise that his enthusiasm for bands with university backgrounds, combined with a deeply intolerant attitude towards phenomena such as Oi!, exposes him as an exponent of class prejudice and petit-bourgeois values.

II
BLOOD SPLATTERED WITH GUITARS
A demonstration of the fact that there are no direct
links between PUNK ROCK, the Sex Pistols and the
Situationist International

PUNK, to paraphrase Howard Devoto, came out of nowhere and was heading straight back there. What was PUNK if not a media hype? It was empty, shallow and trivial – and that was its greatness! When I was fourteen and first got into 'PUNK' in 1976 I didn't know anything about the Situationists, I was too young and ignorant, they wouldn't have interested me. I hadn't even heard of Dada until one of the Sunday papers ran a feature comparing the 'PUNK' phenomenon to events at the Cabaret Voltaire. PUNK was much sound and fury, signifying nothing. After all, what I considered to be PUNK in 1977 turns out to have been a complete misunderstanding, I simply didn't know about genre theory back then. When I was fifteen, loads of people I knew thought *Never Mind The Bollocks Here's The Sex Pistols* was the archetypal PUNK album. Regardless of this fact, its destiny was to become just a dull piece of rock history.

Malcolm McLaren decided to manage the Sex Pistols because he thought they'd be a good advert for his shop. He wanted to sell a lot of trousers! However, things got out of control, because a whole bunch of people decided the rock scene was tired and needed a novelty 'movement' to spruce it up. Of course, there was no master plan, just a lot of confusion and chaos with various individuals working at cross purposes – but that's show biz! Create a scene, but how? Do the Sex Pistols have anything in common with the average PUNK ROCK band? No. Their records were over-produced rock platters and their modus operandi was completely different to that of snotty two-chord garage no-hopers. However, they at least managed to feign ignorance when they started. For example, take a look at *Sounds* of 24 April 1976: 'Who's Sterling Morrison?' asks Steve Jones of the Sex Pistols in an early interview. Well, that blows the Velvet Underground connection! Malcolm McLaren goes on to slag off the New York scene: 'Pretty soon Richard Hell is going to leave the Heartbreakers and Sire Records will dangle a contract in front of him and he knows it won't help and won't do any good, but he'll sign it because it's what's expected of him.'

Hell did leave the Heartbreakers, and did sign a contract with Sire Records. Likewise, as the idea of PUNK took off, it became necessary to create a genealogy for the movement, and the New York scene was the first thing journalists turned up in their search for precedents to the Sex Pistols. Now PUNK is said to begin with the Velvet Underground and as textural proof of this, pretentious morons can cite *From The Velvets To The Voidoids: A Pre-Punk History For A Post-Punk World* by Clinton Heylin (Penguin, London 1993). Heylin recites the laying on of hands through the years as previously rehearsed by lesser lights writing in the weekly rock press, and it goes something like this: Velvet Underground, MC5, Stooges, Modern Lovers, Suicide, New York Dolls, Patti Smith, Television, Ramones, Sex Pistols, Clash. At this point things get a bit sticky if you're a 'serious' rock critic, because it would be embarrassing to endorse anything that wasn't art, right? If you're Greil Marcus you simply whinge on about Elvis Costello and Bruce Springsteen. After this everything is simple because there's U2 and Nirvana. UK Subs? What's that? Something to do with your English tax system?

Rock 'critics', don't you just love 'em? Why is it that publication by Penguin so irreversibly transforms a cynical stringer for a music weekly from an avant-hip satirist into a pretentious bore? As Adam Ant put it in the song *Press Darlings*: 'if passion ends in fashion, then Nick Kent is the best dressed man in town.' Fortunately, most music journalists are incapable of sinking to the depths of imbecility plumbed by Greil Marcus. Heylin's book on American 'PUNK' is anything but a fun read. Nevertheless, he still manages the odd wry quote that puts a smile on your lips and a song in your heart. For example, try this one from Lester Bangs:

> *Rolling Stone* had flown me to [San Francisco to] check me out, since I had been writing for them for about six months. I guess they wanted to see if I was executive limber. I guess I wasn't because not only did I get moved from Greil Marcus's to Langdon Winner's house after about two days, but I thought it was as curious that they sat around not even smoking pot, listening to Mother Earth and Creedence with absolute seriousness...

This is Heylin at his best, putting the boot in without even bothering to elaborate that Marcus went on to 'edit' a collection of Bangs' writing after the hipster died. This, of course, should not surprise anyone since Marcus is a cultural necrophile with a penchant for sucking the blood out of popular culture, as well as indulging in *1984*-style rewritings of history.

It's absurd to suggest that PUNK started with the Velvet Underground because, as I keep saying, as a musical genre it's subject to constant social renegotiation. This text is part of the process and later on I'm gonna unveil a theory of Punk Rock that is so utterly sublime that you won't know whether I'm seriously putting it forward as a means of understanding the subject or just satirising the writing of dickheads like Marcus. However, I can assure you it will demonstrate that I have a much firmer grasp of the movement of modern culture and western philosophical traditions than lumpen-intellectuals such as Marcus. Most of the pretentious twits who are a sandwich short of a hamper and wanna let everybody know it by shouting their absurd 'art' 'rock' 'theories' from the rooftops are content to erroneously trace the origins of PUNK back to some sixties combo. But not Groovy Greil! No sir! Marcus has to compensate for his lack of intelligence by attempting to impress all and sundry with the so called 'ideas' that fester in his brain. Marcus doesn't actually have any thoughts of his own, he simply finds 'his' ideas in other people's books then mangles what he's 'discovered' because this self-styled 'contemporary cultural critic' is incapable of understanding how musical discourse actually functions.

Let me give you an example of this man's idiocy: Aporia Press sent a copy of my book *The Assault On Culture: Utopian Currents From Lettrisme To Class War* to Groovy Greil in 1988, asking him if he'd review it. Marcus responded with a note saying he couldn't possibly review my text because he was writing a book on the same subject! Usually, having done 'research' in the area is understood to be a qualification for passing judgement on a 'similar' work of non-fiction, although grasping this notion proved too great a challenge to the hack in question. I had the misfortune to meet Marcus in 1989, and he was less than pleased with the review of *Lipstick Traces* I'd written for *City Limits*. What a twat! I'd been under instructions from my editor to write something 'fair'. Later, after *New Art Examiner* rang from the States to say that *Lipstick Traces* sucked, deserved a highly critical response and that I was the person to pen it, Groovy Greil was heard blubbering about me to his friends. Marcus didn't understand the graffiti which decorated Paris in May '68 (for example, the slogan 'Be Cruel') although he's written a right load of tosh about it.

Now, let's return to the genealogy Marcus has contrived as his 'history' of PUNK. Groovy Greil has to trace the origins of PUNK back several hundred years earlier than everyone else, thinking this proves how smart he is, when in actual fact, all it does is show him up as a dick. As I keep pointing out, as a musical genre, PUNK has shifting parameters, and lacks a fixed point of origin. However, such a dynamic notion of culture is too much for Marcus to get into his head, besides the name John of Leyden sounds very similar to Johnny Lydon, and so, like one of the maniacs described in Max Nordau's *Degeneration*, our 'contemporary cultural critic' concludes from this that there must be a link between Free Spirit heresies and PUNK ROCK.

At this point, I'd like to parody Groovy Greil's 'critical' method of free association. And so, from Nordau I'm able to move on to Richard Hell, whose notes to the CD reissue of his second album *Destiny Street* are a pale echo of the symbolist 'madness' one of the founding fathers of Zionism attacked in *Degeneration:*

> I am the master of the flaw. Nothing I do is very good, is very talented, but the way I recover from it is exquisite (extraordinary, astonishing, endearing, profoundly endearing, fairly beautiful)... Where did those years go?... Proust, Nabokov... I was insane and desperate and riddled with drugs and lonely and despairing and didn't know how to make a record sound good... Most of my records sound to me like artefacts from a corrupt culture... earnest but inept. They have their charm but you really have to be exceptionally willing – predisposed to sympathy – a scholar of the genre, or to some degree a result yourself of the same forces that produced the 'artist' to really like them, to find beauty in them. At least I think they are brave, they have that poignancy... Sadness rock and roll as a way of turning sadness and loneliness... into something transcendentally beautiful... I'm aware of the utter unredeemable idiocy of apologizing for – denigrating – one's own work. But... I must acknowledge that it is deformed, disturbed, deprived...

Clearly, Hell has spent his entire life on a hiding to nothing. Okay, so he came up with one brilliant plagiarism in *Blank Generation* and one great song with *Love Comes In Spurts,* even the first album was pretty good. However, the bloke was a loser. Unable to take up the past, internalise it and in the process transform it, he simply tried to reproduce the ennui of the 'yellow' 1890s, and like the efforts of his chum Tom Verlaine (the adoption of a French poet's surname by the Television frontman exposes the geezer as

23

an art bore), the results were, on the whole, absurd. Patti Smith was part of the same syndrome, there is a great anecdote about a gig where she was ranting endlessly on the theme of 'great' rock 'n' roll as 'high art', eventually, from the back of the hall someone shouted for *Pictures Of Matchstick Men*, the title of an early recording by the decidedly 'low brow' Status Quo.

Fortunately, back in the mid-seventies, there were bands in New York who had the suss to avoid the bullshit that typified much of the city's club scene, thereby creating a new culture that combined elements of the past with the high energy of contemporary city life. The Electric Chairs, Dictators, Ramones and Dead Boys were all excellent groups, but only in Britain was the conjunction of elements possible that would enable a new generation of rockers to cut through to media overkill! This is where we really have to let go of the music and instead embrace the hype and rhetoric that surrounded it. The protean spawn of the New York club scene was undoubtedly ejaculated into the embryonic London Punk uprising of '76/'77 but there was something else that wouldn't have worked in the 'New World' and that was imagery drawn directly from Britain's repressive and class obsessed society. Suddenly, a monster was stalking the land!

Now don't get me wrong, I'm not trying to suggest that PUNK had a political programme, or even a 'profound' social analysis, it didn't. What PUNK did do was tap into a reservoir of social discontent and create an explosion of anger and energy. PUNK wasn't offering a solution, it was simply a genre of novelty music being hyped on the back of the manic and frequently pointless exploitation of social tensions. PUNK was pure sensation, it had nothing to offer beyond a sense of escape from the taboo of speaking about the slimy reality of life as the social fabric came apart. After all, if Punk Rockers had preferred 'analysis' to 'rhetoric', they'd have been attempting to organise a revolution instead of pogoing to three minute pop songs.

Undoubtedly, it was Steve Jones of the Sex Pistols who uttered the words that inaugurated the 'new wave' explosion. However, Jones was not responsible for Punk Rock, he merely lit the fuse that ignited a fresh outbreak of teenage rebellion. It is impossible to stress too strongly the fact that there was no way a single individual could create the social conditions in which this musical genre flourished. When Jones swore on a tea-time television chat show in

December 1976, I was a fourteen year old who thought it was un-precedented for an ordinary geezer to show the toffs what life was really like. Now I'm older and wiser, on my desk, to one side of a Mac Plus, lies a copy of *Watch Out Kids* by Mick Farren. Inside, there's a reproduction of the front page of the *Daily Mirror* of 9 November 1970. *THE FROST FREAKOUT* screams the headline, *Yippie King puts David on the spot:*

> Television chiefs will begin an inquiry today into the yippie invasion of the David Frost Show. The probe was ordered by Mr. Brian Young, director-general of the Independent Television Authority. It follows the invasion of the Saturday-night programme by about twenty yippies – members of an American revolutionary cult. They swarmed on to the stage while Frost was quizzing yippie leader Jerry Rubin and forced Frost to change to another studio. Some shouted four-letter words and threatened to take over the programme...

Jump forward six years and the headline on the front page of the *Daily Mirror* for 2 December 1976 screams: *THE FILTH AND THE FURY! Uproar as viewers jam phones*. Yes, history repeats itself, the first time as farce, the second as tragedy, only to be absurdly rewritten with a 'Situationist' slant by idiots like Greil Marcus. How-ever, the yippie connection makes a great deal of sense, it brings home what I was saying above about a great many of the wilder aspects of the sixties, and indeed things that were quite openly detested by Debord and his friends, being subsumed under the rubric of Situationism as historians set to work on their task of simplifying the past. Now, the 'truth' of this observation is rein-forced by the fact that I came across the yippie press cutting in Mick Farren's book – a not entirely successful attempt at produc-ing an English version of the 'revolutionary theory' of the Ameri-cans hipsters Abbie Hoffman and Jerry Rubin. Farren was, of course, lead singer with free festival favourites the Deviants, and the chief organiser of the British branch of the White Panthers.

Now the British underground, and in particular the Notting Hill freak scene of the sixties, provide a very strong precedent for late seventies Punk Rock. This should be contrasted with the fallacious notion that there was a vast Situationist input into PUNK. For a start, the Situationist International consisted of a very small num-ber of intellectuals who were consciously organised as a group, whereas both the sixties underground and the PUNK 'movement' were amorphous and disorganised. Secondly, there are innumerable direct connections between the sixties underground and what was understood to constitute British Punk Rock in the '76/'77 period, whereas any connections between Punk Rock and the SI turn out, on examination, to be extremely nebulous.

By tradition, the Situationist-PUNK connection is made through the London based 'revolutionary' group King Mob. However, in order to understand the genesis of King Mob, one needs to know about the Black Mask and Motherfucker groups from the Lower East Side of New York. Black Mask emerged from the New York Surrealist Group and the American Anarchist Group in the mid-sixties. Black Mask's brand of political neo-Dada was of sufficient interest to the specto-Situationists in Paris for the Debordists to consider franchising them as the American section of their organisation. But after a considerable amount of manipulation on the part of Tony Verlaan (a Black Mask fellow traveller, who went on to become a member of the American section of the Situationist International), the Debordists broke with Benn Morea, who was a central figure in both Black Mask and the Motherfuckers. This, in turn, led to the expulsion of the English section of the Situationist International for remaining in contact with Morea. From their early days as the British end of *Rebel Worker*, and then as *Heatwave*, the English section was far closer to the activism of the Black Mask group than the acerbic intellectualism of their French controllers. After their expulsion, the Brits transformed themselves into King Mob with the help of Dave and Stuart Wise who'd moved to London after growing up in Leeds and attending art school in Newcastle. The Wise brothers had already established fraternal links with Benn Morea and were destined to spread huge amounts of bullshit about PUNK ROCK during the eighties in a desperate bid to justify their own past.

Now, since King Mob were clearly an underground phenomena, cast in the same mould as the Motherfuckers, any influence King Mob exerted on Malcolm McLaren and Jamie Reid can hardly be considered 'Situationist'. The Debordists made this state of affairs quite clear in *Internationale Situationiste 12* (translation from *Situationist International Anthology* edited by Ken Knabb, Bureau of Public Secrets, Berkeley 1981), where they stated: 'a rag called KING MOB... passes, quite wrongly, for being slightly pro-situationist'. The SI was self-consciously avant-garde, whereas the wilder aspects of the sixties counter-culture that fed into PUNK bubbled up from a less sectarian, and simultaneously less intellectually rigorous, underground. While the *Black Mask* journal ran odd fragments of Situationist prose translated into English, as *King Mob* would do later, these were reprinted alongside material put out by civil rights organisations and even the Bertrand Russell Peace Foundation! Benn Morea and his group were deeply involved in the anti-Vietnam war movement and developed an analysis of the 'new proletariat' using the slogan 'nigger as class' (a variant on this notion surfaced again in 'connection' to the Sex Pistols when sixties rocker P. J. Proby covered *Anarchy In The UK*, and changed the opening lines from 'I am an anti-Christ, I am an anarchist' to 'I am an anti-Christ, I am a nigger'). While Black Mask and the Motherfuckers succumbed to some, but by no means all, of the illusions prevalent among sixties activists in the US, the flip side of this was that they presented their ideas in an easily accessible, rather than an academic, form. This accessibility led to the flavour of their gestural politics being effortlessly transmitted to the 'blank generation', whereas the acerbic intellectualism of the Situationists was completely alien to the average British teenager in the late seventies.

Besides plagiarising virtually all their graphics from Motherfucker sources, King Mob expended considerable energy in eulogising their chief source of inspiration. For example, from issue 3 of *King Mob*:

> Black Mask seized every possible opportunity of fucking up culture. They moved in at a moments notice and improvised as they went along. They heckled, disrupted and generally sabotaged dozens of art congresses, lectures, exhibitions, happenings. Probably their most notorious escapade was the wrecking of the marathon seminar on Modern Art sponsored by the Loeb Student Centre.. Howls of ART IS DEAD, BURN THE MUSEUMS, BABY and POETRY IS REVOLUTION. Tables kicked over, windows smashed, scuffles breaking out. Larry Rivers roughed up a bit in the best futurist manner. The theoretical dimension – 'fuck off, you cunt' – equally worthy of the occasion.

Greil Marcus prides himself on making connections, but he doesn't mention Black Mask or the Motherfuckers in *Lipstick Traces*, instead he makes the wrong connections. It's a shame Groovy Greil isn't a junkie, because if he'd gone in for that kind of rebel pose, he'd be long dead. However, Marcus does mention King Mob, after all, they are the mythical PUNK-Situationist 'connection', and this is part of what he's got to say about them:

> The group threw a potlatch in Selfridges, with a man dressed up as Santa Claus giving away the department store's toys to throngs of happy children; it accomplished Strasbourg-style detournement when the children were forced to witness the shocking sight of one of Santa's helpers placed under arrest.

Marcus can't, or won't, acknowledge that this prank was first pulled by the Motherfuckers in New York; King Mob simply copied it. Before departing from the subject of King Mob, it's worth noting that Charles Radcliffe, a one time member of the English section of the Situationist International, also pops up in less 'esoteric' histories of the sixties 'rebellion' in Britain. He was an associate of notorious pot smuggler and part-time MI6 man Howard Marks. Charlie ended up with a five year jail sentence for his activities in the dope trade. The English issue of *Rebel Worker*, the precursor to *Heatwave* which in turn begat the English section of the SI and King Mob, is of even greater interest. Under the title *Crime Against The Bourgeoisie*, there is an article on the Who:

> There is a violence in the Who's music; a savagery still unique in the still overtly cool British pop scene. The Who don't want to be liked; they don't want to be accepted; they are not trying to please but to generate in the audience an echo of their own anger... The Who are at full volume; despite predictions of their imminent demise they have two records in the English charts and they will not die until they are replaced by a group offering more far-reaching explosions of sounds and ideas. The Who are symptomatic of discontent. Their appearance and performance alike denounce respectability and conformity... on a good night The Who could turn on a whole regiment of the dispossessed.

And so, rather than providing a link with the Situationists, the King Mob 'connection' takes us back to the Who, an acknowledged influence on the Sex Pistols from their earliest days. And it doesn't matter how long 'contemporary cultural critics' wank in the wind, the Sex Pistols never did cover Velvet Underground songs, while a version of the Who's *Substitute* WAS included in their set.

Likewise the Motherfuckers, via King Mob, were hardly the most immediately accessible aspect of the sixties counter-culture waiting to inspire the average late seventies teenage 'PUNK', while the Situationist 'influence' is completely negligible. What would inevitably be encountered by anyone trailing around the London rock circuit at this date were the musicians and sound crews clustered around the Deviants, the Pink Fairies, the Edgar Broughton Band, Hawkwind etc, all of whom had been stalwarts of the underground free festival scene.

One of the things that tends to be associated with PUNK is independent record labels, not that this was anything new, the idea that it was merely demonstrates the average wo/man's innate capacity for complete amnesia. Nevertheless, independent releases are a quintessential element of the PUNK ROCK phenomenon. In his *New Wave On Record England & Europe 1975-8: A Discographical History* (Bomp Books, Los Angeles 1978), Greg Shaw has the following to say about Stiff Records: 'When punk rock came in, Stiff was quick to get involved with the Damned and others... Stiff was not only the first, but the most successful of the new British labels...' In fact, *New Rose* by the Damned, released on Stiff, is widely considered to be the first single of the British 'new wave' explosion, preceding as it did the release of *Anarchy In The UK* by the Sex Pistols on the major label EMI. Stiff's second release had been *Between The Lines* by the Pink Fairies, and in 1977 they issued a solo single by ex-Fairy Larry Wallis. Likewise, Mick Farren did a comeback EP with Stiff, although for reasons unknown, the label never got around to releasing a planned single by Motorhead, featuring former Hawkwind bassist Lemmy.

Another of the bigger independent labels associated with the British 'new wave' explosion is Chiswick Records, who had the honour of unleashing Motorhead's first single on an unsuspecting world. Chiswick PUNK acts included Johnny Moped, the Radiators From Space, Johnny And The Self-Abusers, and the notorious Skrewdriver in a pre-Nazi incarnation. One of the best punk records of 1977 came out on Chiswick: *I Wanna Be Free* by the Rings. The title was a completely abstract demand, typical of the gestural politics favoured by PUNK and underground bands, the ex-Pink Fairy Twink, now with the Rings, simply demanded freedom in a vacuum. Brilliant – loud, fast and stupid! His next release on Chiswick was *Do It 77,* credited to Twink And The Fairies, presumably because by the time the company got around to issuing the platter in 1978, the appeal of PUNK was waning and they thought they'd do better by cashing in on his underground credibility with a 'punky' revival of an old song. In the eighties, when the company finally released

The Pink Fairies Live At The Roundhouse 1975, they were operating under a variety of label names including Big Beat. It would have been a revelation if Chiswick had released this platter in 1976 or 1977; the tough cockney vocals on *City Kids* are remarkably 'punky' and this is followed by a cover of *Waiting For The Man*, a favourite with '77 PUNK bands such as the Wasps and Slaughter And The Dogs. Clearly, the Velvet Underground had been due a revival and just got lumped in with 'PUNK' because the two things coincided.

Further connections between the British underground and figures associated with the 'new wave' explosion are revealed in the sleeve notes accompanying the track *Psychedelic Music* by the Lightning Raiders on *Back To Front Volume 4*:

> Formed in 1976 by Little John Hodge, Andy Allen and Duncan Sanderson (ex-DEVIANTS and PINK FAIRIES in the sixties) they didn't start to play punk rock before 1979. This is their vinyl debut with Paul Cook and Steve Jones of THE SEX PISTOLS... Andy Allen was also with THE SEX PISTOLS playing bass on their *Great Rock 'N' Roll Swindle* LP. Later he left the Lightning Raiders to join the PROFESSIONALS with Cook and Jones...

Likewise, a 1969 poster promoting the Edgar Broughton Band featured a photo of the group and underneath the legend: 'Wanted – for plotting subversive acts involving treason, arson and corruption of youth...' Ironically, one of the greatest New York PUNK songs of the seventies was recorded by a former yippie and veteran pot smoking street 'musician', this being the title track on David Peel's own label release *King Of Punk* (Orange 1978). The song spits venom: 'I'm the king of punk from the streets of the Lower East suicide... / Fuck you Talking Heads / Fuck you Sex Pistols / Fuck you New York Dolls...' On and on Peel rants, for a glorious seven minutes and seventeen seconds, cursing every New York 'new wave' band of the period: Ramones, Tuff Darts, Television, Blondie etc. With its screaming PUNK ROCK guitars, the track makes a pleasant change from Peel's usual obsessive harping on the themes of dope, uptight pigs and John Lennon.

I hope from what's been said above that it's now clear that rather than being unprecedented, *Anarchy In The UK* was a novelty record in the tradition of Donovan's *Atlantis*. They are two sides of the same coin; hippie mysticism and PUNK nihilism have nothing in common with the 'genuine' revolutionary agitation. This is pop music 'liberating' 'social struggle' from the need to transform anything other than the hit parade. Today, I still find *Atlantis* entertaining, whereas *Anarchy* is so familiar to me that it's dull, there's nothing worse than an over exposed novelty record. The opening line, which struck me as brilliant when I was fourteen, I now view as completely fluffed. Having long ago mastered works such as Max Stirner's *The Ego And Its Own*, I just wish Rotten could have sung 'I am THE Anti-Christ' instead of the half-cocked and absurdly modest 'I am an Anti-Christ'.

The Sex Pistols should have been disposable, instead they've ended up providing the central subject matter for uninspired books by pseudo-intellectuals. It's easy to see why these imbeciles go for the Situationist option when they're confronted with the genealogical question. The Situationist International produced a good number of 'difficult' texts and so they are easy to write about. What one does is explain concepts such as 'the spectacle' or 'detournement'; this fills up a lot of space with less time being put in for the money earned than that required from someone engaging in genuine analysis. The same clichéd incidents are repeated again and again: Notre Dame Cathedral, Strasbourg, May '68, the Pistols at Winterland etc. The assertions of other writers are accepted at face value and no one bothers to examine the circumstances concerning the expulsion of the English section of the Situationist International, thereby unearthing the crucial Black Mask/Motherfucker link.

However, it is at least consoling that the public is smarter than those critics who pretend to be its representatives. The Pistols' greatest problem as a novelty act was always Johnny Rotten, whose expressive voice made him sound like a proper rock singer. After Rotten left the band, the sales of the group's singles soared. Clearly the song *No One Is Innocent*, featuring Great Train Robber Ronnie Biggs on vocals, is vastly superior as a novelty item to *Anarchy In The UK*. While Greil Critic is unable to recognise this, Joe Public proved Hegel to be absolutely correct in the distinction he drew between these two beasts. And in conclusion, let's not forget that it was the part-time Hawkwind member Michael Moorcock who handled the novelisation of the Sex Pistols film *The Great Rock 'N' Roll Swindle*.

31

III
NO MORE ROCK 'N' ROLL
PUNK ROCK discussed as a genre and an
examination of the *Louie Louie* debate

PUNK ROCK is continually splitting in two, the cause of this
bifurcation being swings between a desire for novelty and a
desire for 'authenticity'. In the late seventies, bands like the Clash
were able to make a career on the back of pretending to be somehow more 'authentic' than acts such as the Sex Pistols who'd been
heavily hyped. While the Clash were anything but 'real' (meaning
'unmediated' in a naive rather than a philosophical sense), this
didn't prevent them from projecting a street level image. Indeed,
the fact that Joe Strummer had been to a fee-paying English public school was probably of great assistance when it came to creating
a guttersnipe image for his group. Strummer's lack of contact with
the working class meant that he felt no embarrassment about rein-
venting himself as a caricature of a 'yob'. This resulted in a brilliant debut album marred only by the inclusion of an awful cover
of Junior Murvin's *Police And Thieves*. Unfortunately, the record was
ruined by its corporate sponsor when it finally achieved American
release, with a considerably softened track listing.

One of the major contributing factors to making the first Clash
album such a great record was the fact that the band weren't afraid
to offend by ranting about 'kebab Greeks' in *Hate And War*, or being
'a raving idiot just got off the boat' in *Deny*. Song lyrics of this type
were crucial to the elaboration of a Punk Rock ideology that had
an utterly predictable development. First of all, there were plenty
of people ready and willing to take the rhetoric about class seriously, rather than treating it as the piece of theatre that it so obviously had to be coming from an individual like Strummer. Ultimately, the reductive strategies of the bands that saw working class
'street credibility' as a formula for musical success led to a few idiots upping the level of pseudo-intransigence by going the whole
hog with absurd rhetoric about race, thereby transforming the theatrics of the early Clash into a bestial pantomime. I will deal with
this later.

There is a record dealer I often run into who I've heard say on
more than one occasion that 'if you don't like the Clash, you don't
like rock 'n' roll.' This creature has a huge collection of Clash rari-

ties, and his indiscriminate attitude towards the group makes his pronouncements about music dryly amusing to anyone who's taken the trouble to read a book or two on aesthetics. I can remember going to a party years ago at a rich girl's house (there was a yacht in the front garden and a swimming pool at the back) and complaining about the awful music, only to be told 'but it's the Clash!' I hadn't kept up with the group's rock career and this was the first time I'd heard *Should I Stay Or Should I Go*. I commented that I only liked the group's early records and someone started enthusing about the album *London Calling*. It turned out that nobody else present had heard any of the really early material. However, worse was still to come with *Cut The Crap*, the last Clash album, on which Joe Strummer attempted to return to his 'roots' by making another 'Punk' record. All he succeeded in doing was demonstrating that he'd well and truly lost it.

The Clash were only one side of the English Punk Rock story during the '76/'77 era. Equally good were those novelty records whose 'creators' made no attempt at passing their product off as authentic. One of the greatest punk singles of all time has got to be *Pogo Dancing* by the Vibrators with Chris Spedding. The minimal lyrics rival anything written by the Ramones:

> Hey, this is your chance, to do the pogo dance / So if your feet ain't on the ground, I'll catch you on the way down / Pogo dancing it's the latest thing going around / Why move from side to side when you can jump up and down / Little Suzie had a try / But she jumped so high / That she went over the hill / I hear she's up there still

Released on Mickie Most's independent RAK label in November '76, this classic attempt at exploiting changing musical trends deserved to be a smash but unfortunately it was overshadowed by the Sex Pistols utterly inferior *Anarchy In The UK* – and at the time, even I was bamboozled about the relative merits of the two records. RAK also released the Vibrators anthem *We Vibrate*, another punk classic, before they lost the band to the CBS corporation, who'd also signed up the Clash.

The established pop format of the dance song worked well when enlisted into the evolving novelty genre of Punk Rock. If *Pogo Dancing* played on the relationship between punk and pop then *Do The Robot* – a summer '77 release by the Saints – emphasised that this particular brand of novelty music could also operate within the parameters of the 'rock' genre. Appropriately enough, the Saints had been signed up by EMI subsidiary Harvest on the strength of their debut single *I'm Stranded*, and record company money made it possible for them to relocate from their native Australia to Britain. Their first two albums, *I'm Stranded* and *Eternally Yours*, are brilliant punk platters, while the third – *Prehistoric Sounds* – saw them abandoning this energetic novelty genre in favour of a dull rock sound. After this the band broke up, although singer Chris Bailey went on using the name for his dreadful rock releases. Guitarist Ed Kuepper has had an equally long and uninspired career as a rock musician – both as a solo artist and with the Laughing Clowns. Kuepper, fed up with the way in which Bailey endlessly traded on the glories of their collaborative efforts eventually formed a combo called the Aints. True to the punk spirit, Kuepper was shameless about cashing in on his own past and transformed it into an excellent joke. Perhaps this sense of humour explains why his output has been marginally better than Bailey's since they parted company fifteen or so years ago.

Do The Robot was initially released as one of the two tracks on the B-side of *This Perfect Day* in its 12 inch format. A sticker added to the back of the picture sleeve by the record company states:

> IMPORTANT NOTICE Due to an administrative error, this limited 12" pressing of the Saints' *This Perfect Day* c/w *L-I-E-S* single contains a third, additional title not available on the normal 7" pressing. This additional title, *Do The Robot*, has consequently been withdrawn from future release consideration and will now be available only on this 12" pressing.

This was no more than the usual record company come on to get the punters to part with their cash – and because punk was a novelty genre, the record companies had a field day using gimmicks to flog product. However, it wasn't the corporate record companies who pioneered these scams, they simply tail-ended the independents – Stiff and Chiswick were particularly adept at marketing ploys. Everything was grist to the hip-capitalists' mill; limited editions, coloured vinyl, picture bags, 6 inch singles, 12 inch singles, 10 inch albums, 45 rpm 'albums', scratch 'n' sniff sleeves etc etc. The seventies PUNK ROCK explosion didn't have much impact on the American market, and as a consequence 'new wave' didn't single-handedly reverse the major record labels ailing fortunes. Nevertheless, late seventies PUNK ROCK was of supreme importance to the corporate entertainment industry as an exercise in marketing research and development. In this sense, Punk Rock can be said to have saved the major record labels from collapse.

Do The Robot turns up alongside an alternative take of the same tune under the title *International Robots* among the bonus tracks on the Fan Club CD reissue of *Eternally Yours*. *Do The Robot* is by far the better version of the song because the delivery is deadpan, whereas *International Robots* features laughter and jokey backing vocals. Many journalists fail to appreciate that Punk is a novelty genre because it works best when it is played 'straight', which means that self-styled 'contemporary cultural critics' are free to make fools of themselves by indulging their penchant for literalism. Imagine what someone like Groovy Greil Marcus could do with the 'surreal' lyrics of *Do The Standing Still* by the Table, a 1977 release on Virgin that gives the punk use of the established dance lyric format an 'art' spin. Over a bass line that's as inspired as anything to be found within the Rezillos output, the singer intones the following: 'On my window sill in the morning / I can hear the wild geese calling / Do the standing still.' While this is a catchy song with a good punch line, the rest of the words simply aren't interesting enough to be worth reproducing.

Taking the avant-garde input into Punk seriously is a losers game because while certain musicians may have been 'inspired' by revolutionary cultural movements, what they took from these so called 'precursors' was either a simple sense of anarchic fun or else a po-faced attitude that's worthy of nothing but contempt. I can't think of a single Punk record that does anything with 'ideas' taken from Futurism, Dadism, Surrealism or Situationism which is actually interesting enough to make these anti-institutional cultural formations worth discussing as an influence on this evolving musical genre. Personally, I believe it's worth taking the final chapter of Roger L. Taylor's book *Art, An Enemy Of The People* (Harvester Press, Hassocks 1978) seriously. In *A Warning Of The Corrupting Influence Of Art On Popular Culture*, Taylor demonstrates very convincingly that the intellectualisation of jazz was fundamentally an act of violence on the part of the ruling class, it was a very carefully directed blow designed to cripple the energetic culture of various external opponents of the power elite. Serious culture is in a state of terminal decline and its supporters no doubt see the co-option of Punk Rock as the metaphorical equivalent of a blood transfusion.

Returning to the songs I've been discussing, it's obvious that there's a fundamental difference between *Do The Standing Still, Do The Robot* and *Pogo Dancing,* and singles such as *White Riot* and *Complete Control* by the Clash. While all five tracks fit easily into PUNK as a fluid musical genre, only the two titles by the Clash treat Punk rhetoric with enough 'seriousness' for it to be taken up as a confused and ill-defined ideology. This difference is most easily denoted by saying that while the Vibrators, the Saints and the Table played punk rock at specific periods of their assorted musical careers, until the end of 1978, the Clash played Punk Rock, an individual strand within this musical genre which I will signify through the use of capitalisation.

Punk Rock, despite its shifting parameters, can be treated teleologically, which is something I intend to do within the course of this text. While sticking firmly to the principal that because I'm dealing with a musical genre it isn't possible to fix a definitive point of origin for the Punk Rock discourse, I can give a rough outline of its movement, and from this make predictions about the most likely course of its future development. Ironically, Punk Rock's cousin, punk rock (in lower case), is doomed to eternal repetition. When dealing with it, one experiences no sense of progression. This is at once its glory and its tragedy – while the ideologues scream that *Punk Rock Will Never Die* (the title of a song by the Gonads, a defunct Oi! group led by one time music journalist and now tabloid TV critic Gary Bushell), the truth is that Punk Rock is likely to wither away long before its lower case cousin punk rock. One further refinement is necessary if the distinction I am making is going to be clear: from now on when talking broadly about PUNK ROCK as a musical genre that incorporates both novelty punk rock and ideological Punk Rock, I will indicate that I am doing this by using upper case characters for all eight letters that make up the term.

If the Clash were briefly the premier exponents of Punk Rock, after scraping the bottom of the rock cliché barrel with *Never Mind The Bollocks,* the Sex Pistols unburdened themselves of Johnny Rotten and set about creating some of the greatest punk novelty items since the bubblegum explosion of the late sixties. Not only was *The Great Rock 'N' Roll Swindle* that rare thing, a watchable 'rock 'n' roll' movie in something other than a documentary format, the accompanying soundtrack album was an excellent novelty record. However, the band really hit their peak with the spoken word *Some Product Carri On Sex Pistols,* which is a punk rock classic. The one track that stands head and shoulders above everything else is *Big Tits Over America,* largely the creation of Steve Jones, who remained THE key figure in the band throughout their career. The track is a recording of a Sex Pistols appearance on a Californian radio phone-in, where Jones transforms the proceedings into a farce by swearing and asking most of the female callers – and several males – if they have big tits.

To clarify the distinction I've been making, it's perhaps useful to observe that while the MC5 were a Punk Rock band at the time *Kick Out The Jams* was released, the Stooges were always a lower case punk act. Proceeding on this journey into the past, it thus becomes clear that while the Velvet Underground were never a Punk phenomena, back in the sixties the US produced a whole slew of lower case punk rock bands in the form of the Kingsmen, the Sonics, the Seeds, the Standells, the Litter, the Warlords and the Swamp Rats. Now, it's perhaps possible to observe that punk rock is generally more common than Punk Rock. This is not to say that I consider one form to be superior to the other, although there is a fundamental distinction between the way I consume each subgenre. With punk rock, I tend to laugh *along with* what the band is doing, whereas with Punk Rock (which despite its lack of substance, usually takes itself very seriously in a futile attempt to project an image of intransigent 'authenticity'), I generally laugh *at* the 'musicians'.

One of the ways in which Punk Rock, at least around the 1977 period, projected an image of intransigent 'authenticity' was through a rejection of so called 'Coca-Colonisation', and the use of vague anti-American rhetoric. While there have undoubtedly been American Punk Rock bands, I have already cited the example of the MC5 in the late sixties, towards the end of the seventies, the way in which British bands such as the Clash appropriated the Punk Rock discourse, made it very difficult for the Punk Rock phenomena to flourish in the US. There were, of course, notable exceptions such as the Germs or the Dils but songs like *I'm So Bored With The USA* on the first Clash long player, and the resultant insistence on singing in British regional accents, made it impossible for American groups to project themselves as being at the cutting edge of Punk Rock at that particular point in time. The contrast in attitudes between Punk Rock groups and the less self-conscious punk acts is clearly evident in the title of the second single by schoolboy band Eater, whose *Thinking Of The USA* posits America as a place of mythic fulfilment. The Clash chant 'Move over Starsky for the CIA / Suck on Kojak for the USA,' while Eater sweetly sing 'Lou Reed comes from the USA / Walter Lure comes from the USA / Richard Nixon comes from the USA / Gary Gilmore came from the U-S-A!'

This combination of anti-Americanism and regionalism resulted in late seventies style Punk Rock establishing itself very strongly in the various areas of Europe where a 'minority' language is spoken. One of the most vibrant Punk Rock scenes erupted in Finland, which with its small population and Finno-Ugric language (that is unrelated to Indo-European tongues such as English, German, French, Spanish and Italian) led to a great deal of importance being laid on bands singing in their native tongue. Groups such as Ratsia and Kollaa Kestaa would do Finnish language versions of songs by British acts including the Buzzcocks and the Adverts as well as their own material. While these bands sound great, language did prove a barrier to widespread acceptance and groups such as Briard, who sang in English, have tended to make more of an impact outside Scandinavia and Central Europe. Briard's concise output included a hilarious punk version of *Chirpy Chirpy Cheep Cheep*, as well as excellent originals such as *Fuck The Army*, with a roaring guitar riff that has to be heard to be believed. The band's lyrics are classic sneering punk, for example from *Miss World*: 'You're so fucking clean / I wanna sniff your underwear... I wanna sniff the clothes you wear... Your public image is so unreal / I wonder if you ever masturbate.' Obviously, while some Finnish punk bands sang in English, Finnish Punk Rock was necessarily ranted in the native language, which means it's difficult for me to make very many judgements about the more ideologically 'committed' end of that particular scene.

Returning to Britain, one of the reasons that seventies PUNK ROCK had such an impact in this country was that we lacked the punk tradition which is such an integral part of American popular culture. In the States there is a long history of independent record production, whereas in Britain, from the fifties through to the mid-seventies, with the exceptions of a few maverick operations such as Mickie Most's RAK label, the corporate giants had the market stitched up like a kipper. Prior to the 'new wave' explosion of 1977 there had been no equivalent history of British bands and independent record shops releasing their own product, and so this in itself appeared to be a novelty and created a great deal of interest. Thus, while American regional bands of the sixties had issued their own records in pressings as low as 100 to 500 copies and sold them at gigs, any independent British PUNK release in 1977 was guaranteed sales of ten thousand and upwards as long as the label behind it had the confidence to order such a huge quantity of vinyl. Singles on the bigger independents, such as Step Forward, were selling as many as sixty thousand copies. Naturally, as the novelty wore off, the sales dropped dramatically, but for a brief period the British independent record release was a highly viable commodity.

It might surprise fans of the corporate garbage produced by the likes of U2 and Phil Collins to know that the most successful 'rock' song of all time is the punk anthem *Louie Louie*. Music journalist Dave Marsh has written a book about the song, *Louie Louie* (Hyperion, New York 1993), which is likely to offend any fan of ear-piercing garage rock because within it he reproduces all the reactionary platitudes spouted by the kind of humanist arsehole who thought Live Aid was a good idea. I'm not trying to suggest that Marsh has done his research badly because this isn't the case, in fact many parts of the book are well worth reading, particularly those pertaining to the FBI's interest in the song as a piece of subversion once rumours had spread far and wide that it contained dirty lyrics. This does not, however, mean that I endorse Marsh's abysmal prose style, his pseudo-intellectual bullshit, or the particularly crap line in rhetorical questions and exegesis that he favours. In many ways this tome is a classic argument for physically preventing rock journalists from writing at length about music. What's particularly objectionable about the book is Marsh's overbearing focus on Richard Berry as the 'author' of *Louie Louie*, when in fact the song the R&B star 'originally' wrote is very different to the pop classic of the same name that the insanely restrictive property laws of the so called capitalist 'democracies' treat as the 'work' of a single 'composer'. While I'd be the last person to begrudge Richard Berry the money that lifted him out of the poverty trap, the sentimental way in which Marsh tells the story of how this tunesmith regained the publishing rights to *Louie Louie* (which he'd sold cheaply to raise money for his marriage) reinforces several highly repressive cultural stereo-types.

In many ways, Richard Berry is not the author of *Louie Louie*, at best he is a co-author despite the fact that according to 'copyright law' he is the sole author. Many of the laws framed with specific reference to song-writing were enacted to defend the financial interests of Tin Pan Alley against the threat of the infant gramophone industry. Richard Berry wrote and released a number entitled *Louie Louie*; several years later Rockin' Robin Roberts recorded a raucous cover of the song. The Kingsmen made a particularly inept copy of the cover version. In the process *Louie Louie* was transformed, Berry's soft R&B number became a garage novelty item and an international hit to boot, all on the back of its raw energy and being 'so bad it was good'. The mumbled lyrics which many people misheard as being 'suggestive' facilitated the audience's realisation of its productive role in the creation of culture. Listeners heard whatever they wanted to hear in the song, something that hadn't been possible with the Berry 'original'. The lack of a discernible lyric transformed the 'words' into a mirror for the fantasies, fears and desires of millions of Americans. Likewise, the famous cry of 'let's give it to them, right now!' was missing from the Berry 'original'. This had been the contribution of Rockin' Robin Roberts. But the fact remains that the most important contribution to the reworking of the song was made by the general public rather than a musician. *Louie Louie* was no longer the competent R&B number Berry had written, it had become a monster.

Marsh documents certain developments of the song. He notes that the dirty words become a reality on the Iggy And The Stooges version, recorded live and released semi-legitimately on *Metallic KO*, a kind of apotheosis of punk. Unfortunately, his brain seems to have addled since the days in which he co-founded the rock magazine *Creem*, probably as a result of rubbing by-lines with wankers like Greil Marcus at *Rolling Stone* and listening to garbage produced by the likes of Bruce Springsteen. Marsh suggests on page 165 of his book that '*Louie Louie* as a trope made virtually no appearance during the punk rock heyday and the couple of efforts that found their way to wax (the Bloodclots' 1977 affray, for instance) don't amount to much.' This is a strange comment because what is to date the 'definitive' version of the song was released in the very year Marsh reductively believes was 'the punk rock heyday'. Personally, I find this phrase absurd, the musical genre of PUNK ROCK has such flexible parameters that it is utterly meaningless to talk about it having a 'heyday'. Even more bizarre is the fact that the to date 'definitive' version of *Louie Louie* is not to be found in the discography that concludes Marsh's book, in fact, it is not mentioned anywhere in his tome. Marsh appears never to have heard of, let alone heard, the version of *Louie Louie* by John The Postman's Puerile released on Manchester's Big Bent Records circa 1977.

John The Postman was a well known face on the Manchester PUNK scene, 'famous' for getting up onto the stage of the Electric Circus after the bands had played and in an inebriated state, giving renditions of *Louie Louie*. On the back of this, someone decided to let the Postman, and his backing band Puerile, loose in a recording studio to make an album. Naturally, one side is taken up with two renditions of *Louie Louie*, credited on the label, which the consumer is expected to cut out of a larger sheet and then glue onto the record, as *Louie, Louie, (version)* and *Louie, Louie, (slight return VOL. 7.....)*. *Louie, Louie, (version)* takes the amateurism of the Kingsmen to its logical conclusion with grossly incompetent musicianship and a drummer who seems to be experiencing extreme difficulty simply keeping time. Instruments stop and start and the song goes on and on, while over the top of this cacophony, John The Postman sings the chorus and then whatever comes into his head instead of the original words:

> You're gonna have to listen to this / For the next fifteen minutes or less... I hate the door / And I hate the window / And I hate you all / Looking at me now... You're coming up to the middle section / And we're gonna keep it beyond your comprehension...

This is the destruction of Berry's 'original' song, begun by the Kingsmen, taken to its logical conclusion. *Louie, Louie, (slight return VOL. 7.....)* is marginally more competent but it still makes the Kingsmen sound like Led Zeppelin. It probably won't surprise those not already in the know that John The Postman's next release was an equally long and shambolic rendition of *Gloria*.

There are other 'important' punk covers of *Louie Louie* missing from both Marsh's discography and his book. Take, for instance, the Angry Samoans, whose June 1981 set at the 700 Club in New York concluded with a version of *Louie Louie*. This was released posthumously as part of *Return To Samoa* by Shakin' Street in 1990. Without doubt, the Angry Samoans were one of the best West Coast punk bands of the early eighties, with short catchy songs and the ability to get right up the noses of the music business establishment. Perhaps the group's greatest achievement was *Get Off The Air*, a character assassination of LA DJ Rodney Bingenheimer. The radio personality made himself look like a complete jerk by threatening legal action over lines such as:

> He can't read / Baby he can't walk / He's LA's favourite punk rock jock / Glitter bands and Bowie's cock / Are his ideas of new wave rock / You're just a fucking piece of shit now Rodney / I don't think you're so hot / You make me laugh with those clothes you wear / And those lame brain teeth you've got / 8pm and Rodney's on the air / He's beating off in Joan Jett's hair / Christmas Eve and what have you got? / Four hours of Phil Spector rot / Get off the air / Get off the air you pathetic male queer / You don't impress me / Get off the air / You're just a jerk as far as I can see.

Homophobia recurred frequently in the Angry Samoans lyrics, to such an extent that it became a fixation. The group's sneering attitude towards the musical establishment and straight society in general was something they were only able to match in sheer intensity with these obsessive references to a love that dare not speak its name. Whether or not the band were ever able to give physical expression to these urges, there can be little doubt that they knew the etymological origins of the term PUNK and that the frisson this created gave them quite a thrill. The Angry Samoans managed to combine their two major interests yet again on a reworking of their song *Steak Knife*, which they retitled *Posh Boy's Cock*. For the benefit of those not already in the know, Posh Boy was the name of an LA based punk rock record label, and the lyrics ran: 'If you wanna make a record / if you wanna rock / Just grab a hold of Posh Boy's cock / Three big inches long and mean / Posh Boy's cock is on the scene.'

Such tortured expressions of sexual desire are common among the more 'guttersnipe' brands of PUNK ROCK, and relate very closely to the pleasures and pains associated with rituals of male bonding. This can be witnessed not only in song lyrics but also in the mock violent interaction of the audience occupying the pit immediately in front of the stage at PUNK ROCK concerts. While, as should be clear from what I've already stated, this form of sexual expression is rarely given open verbal articulation outside that particular strand of Punk Rock known as Queercore, such boundaries are occasionally crossed by individuals who are less confident about defining their own sexuality but nevertheless feel compelled to address the issue because their ideological beliefs necessitate the transgression of all social norms. The fact that the Angry Samoans did not come out of the closet is one of a number of factors that led me to the conclusion they were a punk rock, and not a Punk Rock, band.

One band not afraid of addressing this issue were the London based Apostles, although they made no attempt to resolve the contradictions which they presented to their audience. The Apostles operated on the fringes of the anarcho-'punk' scene, but were never really integrated into it because their Punk Rock attitude prevented the ideology they'd adopted from becoming coherent enough to be acceptable to their apparent peers in the Conflict/Crass/Poison Girls camp. Songs such as *Fucking Queer* won the band few friends:

> Boots and braces in nineteen seventy-six / Some of us had knives others carried sticks / Oppressed with guilt and fear looking for a fucking queer / Clapham Common was our training ground / We'd kick that fairy in when no one was around / We had to make it clear we were not fucking queer / It seems so long ago when we were real men / Memories linger on I feel guilt now and then / For one day I awoke my thoughts no longer dim / I met this strange young lad and fell in love with him / And so I realise while I'm laying here / The truth that I despise that I'm a fucking queer.

Several records and a couple of years later, the Apostles followed this up with a 1984 EP entitled *The Giving Of Love Costs Nothing*. The platter showed that the band were still prepared to address sexual issues but the way in which they did so lost them most of the few friends they'd made along the way. One side of the record featured what appears to be a gay love song and a rant against bigotry, the flip contradicts this with tracks entitled *Rock Against Communism* and *Kill Or Cure*. The lyric to the latter song runs as follows:

> They walk the streets at night / A pathetic sight to see / A product of our sick society / Earls Court and Piccadilly / Hanging round toilets all night long / Thank God they stay away from me / Kill, kill, kill or cure / Kill, kill, kill or cure / Or put them all out of their misery.

While the so called anarcho-'punk' groups weren't really playing Punk Rock at all, because notions of ideological coherence came to dominate their thinking and these were reflected in every aspect of their activity, the Apostles were locked into a rigid Punk Rock groove where a desire to explore contradictory impulses resulted in stasis if not actual paralysis. Conflict, Crass and the Poison Girls reached a huge audience, many of whom considered themselves to be 'Punks', but as I've already pointed out, they'd been left behind by the Punkgeist whose dialectic was very different to that of anarcho-pacifism. While the Apostles remained true to the spirit of Punk, this was very much in the form of a return at a lower level. The schizophrenic attitude of the band made it impossible for them to move in any direction whatsoever, unless this was done in a completely tentative fashion and quickly negated by some contradictory action. As a form of discourse developed to a large extent by teenagers, Punk 'progressed' very much through the transformation of quantity into quality. What was required was a push in a single direction until changes in quantity became a change of quality, just as raising the temperature of water eventually transforms it into steam. I shall return to this theme later.

IV
RELICS FROM THE PAST
British PUNK ROCK circa 1977

Before getting to grips with the dialectical transformations of Punk Rock, I want to deal with a particular moment in the history of PUNK ROCK that was a time of both fusion and division. This is the period when the legacy of sixties garage rock became completely entangled with the ideology of Punk Rock passed down to a subsequent generation by the likes of the MC5. Indeed, quite a number of intellectually unsophisticated writers would lead you to believe that the genesis of PUNK ROCK is to be found in this period. However, as I've already pointed out, as an evolving musical genre, PUNK ROCK has no fixed boundaries. 1977 is only one of many points at which we could begin to investigate this phenomenon. Those pseudo-intellectuals who believe that it is possible to discover the 'origins' of Punk Rock at this particular juncture in the development of the discourse have quite simply failed to grasp the dynamics of culture and their 'work' should be subjected to merciless criticism.

1977, at least in the way it was mythologised by the Clash on the flip-side of their first single *White Riot*, was a time of apocalypse. However, this was not the only vision of what that year was about, according to the brief sleeve notes on the back of a Beggars Banquet compilation album entitled *Streets: Select Highlights from Independent British Labels:*

> 1977 was the year that the music came out of the concert halls and onto the streets; when independent labels sprang out of the woodwork to feed new tastes; when rock music once again became about energy and fun; when the majors' boardrooms lost control. Suddenly we could do anything.

Clearly, while the Clash were projecting themselves as the epitome of Punk Rock, *Streets* is basically about punk rock. However, the distinction is somewhat opaque because a handful of the tracks on the *Streets* compilation reflect vague social concerns that could be subsumed under the nebulous ideological posturing of Punk Rock. *Cranked Up Really High* by Slaughter And The Dogs appears, from what it's possible to decipher of the lyrics, to be an anti-drugs song. Other contributions from Manchester, such as *Ain't Bin To No Music School* by the Nosebleeds and *Lookalikes* by the Drones, also give

45

the impression that the bands may be participating in some barely articulated form of social protest. Marginally more impressive in terms of political content is the anti-fascist anthem *Fear On The Streets* by the Members. Coming from, or possibly going in, the opposite direction is *Arabs In 'Arrads* by the Art Attacks, with its catchy chorus of 'Hungry in the food hall / Staring at the salmon / I can't compete with the Arabs in 'arrads'. Likewise, *Disastermovie* by the Exile could be seen as a Punk Rock stab at populist politics with its plea of 'Let's all join together / Give the country a second look!'

Several ditties on *Streets,* all lacking any consciously articulated ideological dimension, will be found distasteful by the political correctness brigade. *College Girls* by Cane with its chorus of 'Every guy knows how juicy they are / Oh oh college girls clits,' is a classic slice of punk rock. The Drive contribute a song about masturbation entitled *Jerkin'*, and the Pork Dukes offer *Bend And Flush*, the punk rock equivalent of a smutty music hall song. *Be My Prisoner* by the Lurkers is unlikely to go down well with those reactionary elements within the feminist movement who are opposed to consensual sado-masochism, while *isgodaman* by Arthur Comics? appears calculated to upset Christians as well as being very funny indeed.

Since PUNK ROCK is all about acne splattered youth having a go at sitting targets, both musically and lyrically, *Streets* is an excellent example of the genre. If we examine other tracks by the groups featured on the record it becomes obvious that most of them fit more neatly into the punk rock, as opposed to Punk Rock, category. All the songs featured on the record were recorded in 1977, a time at which an explosion of media interest in PUNK ROCK led to a great deal of confusion about substrands within the genre. However, while genre categorisations are necessarily provisional, it's not a difficult task to untangle the current standing of the songs and acts to be found on the *Streets* compilation.

It seems like a good idea to reiterate here that there are basically three strands to what we are disentangling – music, lyrics and image. Music is probably the least important aspect in terms of drawing a distinction between punk rock and Punk Rock, since both tend towards the harder end of the pop format with a propensity for tuneful two to three minute songs. Music is more useful as an aid to exploring the differences between PUNK ROCK and those strands of the broader pop and rock genre that are sometimes

confused with it. For example, by ignoring the PUNK emphasis on
tuneful pop melodies, even if these were buried beneath guitar
distortions, hardcore and so called anarcho-'punk' bands created
new rock subgenres that are completely distinct from PUNK ROCK.
Lyrically, the anarcho-pacifist bands were also far too specific and
articulate in giving vent to their social concerns, whereas Punk Rock
politics are notoriously vague, or if at all specific, so absurd that
they indicate those involved have had little qualitative contact with
organised ideological groupings. Finally, while Punk Rock groups
are more concerned with projecting a 'street level' image than punk
rock bands, the way this posturing was taken up within hardcore
and anarcho-'punk' became so caricatured and stereo-typed that it
was transformed into a mutant brand of bohemianism, something
completely alien to PUNK ROCK as a form of popular culture.

Returning to the *Streets* compilation, let's look first at *Fear On
The Streets* by the Members, the most obvious candidate for inclusion in the Punk Rock canon. While there is no reason why this
song, taken in isolation from the rest of the group's output (or
possibly even coupled with the raucous B-side *GLC*) should not be
considered an example of Punk Rock, anyone who views the Members entire career can see that over the course of a few years they
transformed themselves from a punk rock group to a moderately
successful pop act (they had the odd hit single).

Both live and on record the Members stressed the pop aspect of
their brand of punk rock by laying great emphasis on novelty and
humour. Apart from anything else, this was a 'natural' course for
them to follow because they looked odd; singer Nicky Tesco was
short enough to be considered a metaphorical, if not a literal,
midget. Song titles such as *Soho A Go Go* and *Love In A Lift* reveal
the music hall origins of their smutty humour, while other tracks,
most explicitly *Chelsea Nightclub*, contain passages of musical pas-
tiche in homage to sixties pop, in this case self-consciously drawing out the element of youthfulness in both PUNK and Mod by
plagiarising the Who's *My Generation*. However, although the group
dubbed their music the *Sound Of The Suburbs* (they came from
Camberley in Surrey, in easy commuting distance of London), they'd
absorbed enough of the Punk spirit to record the odd serious song
such as *Fear On The Streets* or the awful white reggae of their hit
single *Offshore Banking Business*.

The other groups featured on *Streets* who went on to make the British pop charts are the Doll and the Lurkers. The Doll's contribution to the record, *Trash*, was by far and away the best track they ever recorded, owing as it does – both in terms of music and the sneering lyrics – a huge debt to sixties garage rock. The Lurkers are much more interesting than the Doll, having had a long career full of interruptions and line-up changes. In the late seventies, the group were peddling a souped-up version of pub rock and quickly gained a huge Skinhead following, thanks to their no nonsense attitude towards music. Again, song titles such as *I'm On Heat* reveal the roots of the band's very British humour in music hall traditions. Having broken up and reformed a couple of times, the Lurkers released their classic surf-punk mini-album *King Of The Mountain*, on Link in 1989. This was followed by the tuneful *Powerjive* and *Non-Stop Nitropop* long players on Released Emotions and Weser respectively. The Lurkers more recent recordings demonstrate that punk bands don't necessarily get worse as they get older, although live performances have been marred by Arturo Bassick's seriously sad banter with the audience, which has been known to degenerate to the level of 'I'm 37 years old and I still believe in Punk Rock!'

In terms of cult status, Slaughter And The Dogs stand head and shoulders above everyone else featured on *Streets* as the classic punk rock act. They went on to record the anthem *Where Have All The Boot Boys Gone?* and the *Do It Dog Style* album for Decca. The band appeared desperate to make the charts, as well as having one of the most muscular stage acts to be seen on the college, pub and club circuits in the late seventies. Live they were awesome, but singer Wayne Barrett's relationship with a Paris based chick caused the group to break up before they succeeded in reaching a mass audience. The band reformed in 1979 but Barrett was soon replaced by Ed Banger, formerly lead singer with the Nosebleeds, for the competent rock album *Bite-Back*.

Unfortunately, *Bite-Back* wasn't quite as much fun as bassist Howard Bates and guitarist Mike Rossi's ill-fated attempt to court the teeny-bopper market as the Studio Sweethearts. Nevertheless, the Dogs' shamelessness in switching image and attempting to tail-end any and every trend, demonstrated they were true punks who paid no heed to the empty rhetoric of their peers, many of whom were prone to wanking on about artistic integrity. Barrett and Rossi reformed the band yet again in 1991 for another stab at the mainstream rock market with the *Shocking* long player. Not even an abysmal attempt at dealing with the 'serious' subject of ecology, in the shape of the song *Stop Playing With Mother Earth*, could ruin Slaughter And The Dogs cult status as one of the greatest punk bands of all time. In this particular genre tackiness is greatness, and the Dogs are as cheap and nasty as they come!

When it comes to plumbing the depths, few punk musicians could sink as low as Mike Rossi, who played guitar on the unlistenable *Sing It To Me* platter, which is co-credited to him and Gary Holton. Rossi also provided accompaniment on Martin Degville's *World War Four*, a hilarious solo outing by the former Sigue Sigue Sputnik bod. Another 'must have' for fans of punk trash is the Mike Rossi interview disk that was given away free with one pressing of Slaughter And The Dogs *Live At The Factory*. On this, the hapless guitarist leaves the listener with the impression that he's got nothing but air between his ears and proves conclusively that the average musician has nothing of interest to say about whatever classic tunes s/he happens to have recorded. Mike Rossi is a complete loser, and this makes him a PUNK STAR, the ideal candidate for a 'new wave' version of *This Is Your Life*!

Among PUNK record collectors, the only other band featured on *Streets* who come anywhere close to matching the cult status of Slaughter And The Dogs are the Drones. This group were a competent live act whose standout studio recordings are *Lookalikes, Just Want To Be Myself* and *Bone Idol*. Their only album, *Further Temptations*, is a solid example of high octane garage rock although it doesn't really stand up to repeated listenings. The group is heard to best effect on the *Short Circuit: Live At The Electric Circus* compilation, where their contribution *Persecution Complex* is considerably better than the studio version of the same song. However, the Drone's real claim to fame is as a skeleton in the closet of media personality Paul Morley, who broke into the music business by acting as the group's manager.

The Art Attacks provide an example of how misleading it can be to judge a band by a single track on the *Streets* compilation. Led by cartoonist Savage Pencil, the group were an outlet for his comic vision of life. In fact, with the exception of humourless political hacks and 'contemporary cultural critics', it will be obvious to most listeners that *Arabs In 'Arrads* is a vehicle for the Art Attacks' bleak humour and isn't intended to be racist or offensive. This is apparent not only from the singer/cartoonist's artwork on the sleeve of the *Streets* album but also from songs such as *Rat City* with its almost unconscious parody of Lou Reed's *Waiting For The Man*: 'Feeling sick / Feeling bad / Go get yourself a donor kebab'. *Rat City* was recorded in May 1977 and demonstrates that New York and London are worlds apart aesthetically as well as geographically:

> Razor blade in the palm of your hand / A bomb goes off on the underground... Snipers on the Post Office Tower / Just waiting for their final hour / In Rat City, it's so shitty... Going on the tube to work / Just getting out and going into my office and sitting round there / And all I ever do is get a load of crap thrown at me / And the only pleasure I ever get is watching the secretaries legs, you know / And what do I do? / I get out, I put on my coat / I walk out and then I grab myself a drink / And then I find myself getting so pissed, I just don't know what to do / And so I walk out and walk about the street / And I sort of slip into one of those greasy sex cinemas / There's nothing on but a load of shit like a Swedish porn movie / Everything in it / It just doesn't work for me / It isn't real / It's like Rat City, it's so bad / I can't get anything to eat in it / I've got to get home but I'm so pissed I can't / So I go home and the wife says 'Hey where the hell have you been?' / I said 'I I' / And she says 'Well your tea's ready and it's fish fingers again!'... I can't stand fish fingers / So I eat 'em and I have a couple of glasses of beer again and I watch TV / But there's nothing on except *Police Woman*... Rat City, it's so shitty.

Nothing else the Art Attacks did was able to explode social realism in quite the same way but the whole of their concise output is worth hearing. Apart from the two numbers already discussed, the only other songs to find their way onto vinyl were studio recordings of *I Am A Dalek, Neutron Bomb* and *Punk Rock Stars*, plus two tracks – *Animal Bondage* and *Frankenstein's Heartbeat* – on the *Live At The Vortex* compilation album. Although the Art Attacks' aesthetic is unmistakably English, their music is archetypal of late seventies PUNK ROCK from anywhere in the Western world. For example, on *Punk Rock Stars* Savage Pencil rhymes 'movie' and 'groovy', something Australian band the Saints do on their song *Private Affair*. Likewise, *Neutron Bomb* was also used as a song title by West Coast punk acts the Controllers and the Weirdos. Nuclear apocalypse is a common theme in PUNK ROCK, although here Savage Pencil pulls off a neat twist on it by threatening to use advanced technology to annihilate his girlfriend's family and neighbours.

Another act on *Streets* with a typically English sense of humour were Arthur Comics?, better known as the Snivelling Shits. Led by music journalist Giovanni Dadamo, the group's limited output included *I Can't Come*: 'I guess I really fooled you all I was using my thumb / The truth of the matter is I can't come.' The lyric has been described by its author as: 'The Shits answer to *Satisfaction*. Warning: taking drugs can seriously damage your genitals.' Other punk classics by the combo include *Only 13*, in which Dadamo describes how being picked up on the tube by an old lecher led him to discover a new way of earning money, and *Terminal Stupid*: 'Terminal stupid your head's in a mess / I can count your brain cells on one finger or less.'

Even more reductively fixated on bodily functions than the Snivelling Shits, and represented on *Streets* by their first single *Bend And Flush*, were the Pork Dukes. The group's song titles are indicative of their interests and humour: *Dirty Boys*, *Stuck Up*, *Sick Of Sex*, *Down Down Down*, *Soho Girls*, *Tight Pussy*, *Big Tits* or *Penicillin Princess*. Their second single, *Making Bacon*, provides a typical example of the Dukes' use of rhyming couplets sung in an outrageously camp voice: 'Get down baby on your hands and knees / Take my Danish and give it a squeeze.' Naturally, this outrage came in a twelve-inch format on yuckie yellow vinyl. The album that followed had a plain white sleeve with a few brightly coloured stickers added to spruce it up, among the messages on these were: 'FOR A REAL GOOD TIME WHEN IN LONDON, PHONE THE PORK DUKES FAN CLUB ON 01-203 1750 AND ASK FOR SUZI!'

If I've spent a good deal of time dealing with the *Streets* compilation that's because it's the best contemporary jumping off point for dealing with the wide expanse of late seventies British punk rock. If I now begin to move away from the acts featured on *Streets*, this is by no means because I've exhausted what I've got to say about them. Obviously, I could talk about the classic Exile track *Fascist DJ* from their *Don't Tax Me* EP, or how *Disaster Movie* was ultimately issued by Charly Records as a maxi-single alongside *The Real People* and *Tomorrow Today*. Likewise, I could compare the merits of *Jerkin'* by the Drive with its flip-side *Push 'N' Shove*, which achieves sublimity by rhyming 'loving' and 'shoving'. However, I am not attempting an exhaustive catalogue of my subject precisely because idiotic feats of this type are regularly attempted by anally retentive record collectors who have no understanding of the evolving nature of musical genres, or how the dynamics of the PUNK ROCK discourse makes such an exercise not only impossible but also thoroughly pointless.

In 1977 the compilation *Live At The Roxy London WC2* appeared to me to be an archetypal PUNK artefact. These days, I've changed my opinion; despite the clips of audience babble between the tracks the record is too sanitised. The thing kicks off well enough with two songs by Slaughter And The Dogs, *Runaway* and *Boston Babies*. Next up are the relatively obscure Unwanted, whose studio recordings *(Withdrawal, 1984, Bleak Outlook, Secret Police, These Boots Are Made For Walking, I'm Not Me, Fraulein* and *The End Is Nigh)* achieve moments of 'greatness' without ever scaling the heights they reached with their first ever performance immortalised on the *Roxy* album. *Freedom* is the band's masterpiece, a moronic couple of minutes that stands up against all comers within the genre. This is followed by two contributions from Wire, a fine band in their own right but the group's offerings are art rock not PUNK. After this there's the usual lame outing from the Adverts, who were always awful live but somehow managed to lay down a few decent tracks in the studio despite the handicap of singer TV Smith's insane over-estimation of his extremely limited intellect. Things improve with Johnny Moped and Eater, the latter band being a bunch of schoolboys who later took the sneering punk rock attitude to its logical conclusion with their anthem *Get Raped*. Unfortunately, Eater are followed by X-Ray Spex who give novelty records a bad name. The album closes with two tracks from the Buzzcocks, a great pop group but they ceased playing Punk Rock when they parted company with original singer Howard Devoto.

PUNK ROCK is a receding object; as one approaches, it disappears. In this genre obscurity, despite the fact that it is necessarily relative, is everything. Since PUNK ROCK at the time of its production is initially consumed by a relatively young audience, we should not expect subtlety from those engaged in the discourse. Part of the reason *Live At The Roxy* now seems so unsatisfactory as a PUNK ROCK artefact is that the majority of the bands featured on it are so well known within the genre. A follow up release, *Farewell To The Roxy*, is a considerable improvement on its predecessor because it features such lesser known acts as Blitz, Acme Sewage Co., Billy Karloff & The Goats, UK Subs, Tickets, Red Lights, XL5, Jets, Streets, Plastix, Bears, Open Sore and the Crabs.

Undoubtedly, the standout tracks on *Farewell To The Roxy* are *Sniper* by the Streets and *Fun Fun Fun* by the Bears. *Sniper* consists chiefly of the word 'sniper' chanted over a very Who-ish riff, circa *I Can't Explain*, classic minimalistic stuff. *Fun Fun Fun* is heads down, no nonsense, mindless punk rock boogie and that's its joy. The lyrics say it all: 'I'm gonna go down to the shop / Buy some flour and some eggs / Then I'll go to the top of the flats / And drop them on your head / Gonna have fun fun fun and we've only just begun...' Any idiot who believes that PUNK ROCK is profound ought to be forced to listen to this track repeatedly for a week – or at least until they cackle madly, get down on their hands and knees, then howl at the moon. This is what rock 'n' roll is about, mindless youthful exuberance.

The main disappointment on *Farewell To The Roxy* is the Crabs contribution. One expects something a bit better than a punk lullaby from a band whose merchandising operation consisted of a T-shirt emblazoned with the slogan 'I CAUGHT THE CRABS'. This compilation should have featured their stage favourite *Victim*, but then a studio version came out as a single on Lightning who also issued the second *Roxy* long player. The one other band on the platter who are particularly worthy of note are the UK Subs, who in the course of a long career went on to much greater things than these live renditions of *Telephone Numbers* and *I Live In A Car*. Despite being old enough to have fathered the average teenage PUNK ROCKER, lead singer Charlie Harper had a seriously juvenile attitude and became a 'new wave' face. This is the man who authored such classic chorus lines as 'dirty girls go yeah yeah yeah' and 'all I wanna know, all I wanna know, is does she suck?' A career as a PUNK musician had obvious attractions to a man of Harper's tastes.

However, since the boundaries of any particular genre are constantly being renegotiated, in assessing what constituted British PUNK ROCK in the late seventies it is necessary to look at more than merely contemporary artefacts. A good example of the retrospective PUNK ROCK compilation, unconstrained by the niceties of our insanely restrictive copyright laws, is the 1990 bootleg CD *Anarchy In The UK Volume One*. It should go without saying that Volume Two never appeared. The CD features Swell Mob, the Users, Menace, Visitors, Drones, Rikki And The Last Days Of Earth, Astronauts, the Exits, Blitzkrieg Bop, Eater, Y Yrwynau Coch, Vice Creems, Wasps, Bleach Boys, Accidents, Le Ritz and the Now. The man behind the bootleg appears to be utterly shameless, since the inclusion of tracks by the Users and the Now alongside an advert for the defunct *Spiral Scratch* magazine, are obvious clues to his identity. On the other hand, since it would have been virtually impossible to trace some of the copyright holders, few of whom were likely to initiate legal action, this particular impresario probably doesn't have much to worry about.

As an early 'minority' language PUNK ROCK record, the *Recordiau Sgwar* EP by Y Yrwynau Coch, from which *Ail Ddechre* is lifted, was a crucial moment in the development of Welsh youth culture. However, to listeners who don't speak the language, it merely sounds like a pleasant punk/pop song. Of more interest from my particular perspective are the two tracks taken from the Exits *Yodelling* EP. The first, *Apathy*, by its very name reveals a classic PUNK ROCK obsession which rose to even greater prominence in England during the late seventies, at a time when the subgenres of punk rock and Punk Rock had become hopelessly entangled. Since the Buzzcocks had already used the title *Boredom* for a track on their seminal *Spiral Scratch* EP, other bands were left consulting the thesaurus for synonyms. The Exits bagged one of the better options. Base 3, whose only release was the single *Fast Train To China*, never got around to committing their song *Monotony* to vinyl, and in any case they'd been beaten to the punch by the Boys who included a track with this title on their fourth album *Boys Only*. Somehow synonyms such as 'Indifference', 'Ennui', Doldrums' and 'Listlessness' just didn't sound PUNK enough. This left everyone else scratching around for variations on the key word. Martin And The Brownshirts came up with the not very inspired *Boring,* which was the flip to their 24 carat punk classic *Taxi Driver.* Returning to the Exits, the other song that's been bootlegged from their *Yodelling* EP, *Glandular Angela,* is also prototypically punk. The chorus line of 'I've got a fever for your beaver', exposes us yet again to the ongoing punk rock obsession with smutty music hall traditions and cheap novelty lyrics.

Rikki And The Last Days Of Earth actually made an album for DJM, the lame *4 Minute Warning*. Their public school background is obvious to the attentive listener in the lyrical content of songs such as *Aleister Crowley*:

I'm Aleister Crowley – Aleister Crowley / You know my number –
you know my name / The chains of lust round my picture frame /
I'm Aleister Crowley – tolling the bell / I'm Aleister Crowley – at
the gates of hell / The mark of the Beast – you can plainly see /
The powers of darkness – all work for me.

Sad, very sad, the boys had no street credibility, and come across
like the novelistic nonentities Martin Amis and Will Self with guitars and keyboards. Nevertheless, *City Of The Damned*, the group's
best single which is bootlegged here, does the business, which is a
lot more than can be said for anything else they recorded. Fortunately, Eater and the Drones, the only other acts on the *Anarchy In
The UK* CD to record albums, acquitted themselves with dignity,
producing long players that could be listened to without ruining
their two or three minutes of glory.

Menace sit least easily on the compilation, despite being represented by their best single *GLC*, because their hardheaded brand
of Punk Rock was a very important tributary feeding into that
substrand of the genre which went on to transform itself into Oi!
whereas everyone else can be subsumed under the heading of punk
rock. Of course, the bootleg also features the obligatory band led
by a music journalist, in this case the Vice Creems, featuring Kris
Needs of Zig Zag. The Vice Creems' *Danger Love* is an acceptable
slice of poppy punk but lacks the punch of Swell Mob's *Violence*,
which not only features a punked up *Matthew And Son* riff, it also
boasts the chorus line: 'violence, violence, it's the only thing that
makes sense!' Just as good is *Chloroform* by the Bleach Boys, who
suggest that abusing the substance featured in the title of their
song is a lot more fun than sniffing glue. Nothing less than a punk
novelty classic! Despite singing in American accents, the Users from
Cambridge achieved cult status with their first single *Sick Of You*
backed with *(I'm In Love With) Today*. Their second release *Kicks In
Style* is bootlegged on *Anarchy In The UK*.

The CD also features both sides of the Wasps first single *Teenage
Treats* coupled with *She Made Magic*, which aren't bad but don't hold
a light against the first of their two tracks on the *Live At The Vortex*
compilation. *Can't Wait 'Til 78* was a great way to up the stakes in
the game of PUNK brinkmanship, while everyone else was still attempting to show how 'with it' they were by singing about 1977,
the Wasps were looking forward to the following year. It's just a
shame that their other contribution to the *Vortex* album was a cover

of Lou Reed's *Waiting For The Man*. Equally disappointing was the single *Rubber Cars*, backed with *This Time*, on the major RCA label. There's a great deal more that could be written about the PUNK ROCK genre in Britain in 1977 but it would be counterproductive to adopt the list as an organising principle and insist on reproducing the titles of all my favourite PUNK ROCK songs from this geographical location and period. All I wanted to do by discussing various compilations of late seventies British PUNK ROCK was indicate both the broad range of material being discussed, and simultaneously reiterate that the boundaries of the genre are anything but fixed. The choice of period and geographical location was to an extent arbitrary, although the fact that I possess a detailed first hand knowledge of the material reviewed above obviously biases me towards this particular segment of the genre.

In the past it has been all too easy for individuals writing about PUNK ROCK to avoid any attempt at defining the subject by adopting a 'common sense' approach. The line generally taken by 'contemporary cultural critics' and other idiots is that everyone 'knows' the Sex Pistols and the Clash played 'PUNK ROCK'. By dealing with groups whose output isn't found in the average high street record shop, we not only get to grips with material that is more typical of the genre, we begin to see 'common sense' notions of PUNK ROCK falling apart. Indeed, it becomes clear that contrary to 'common sense', the Sex Pistols did not, in fact, make PUNK ROCK records.

Having said this, I do not want to deny the importance of the Sex Pistols as an inspiration to many of the groups discussed in this text. A mythic notion of the activities engaged in by Malcolm McLaren and his protégés provided an important organising principle for many of the groups mentioned in previous pages. However, this does not mean that the Sex Pistols, or other figures such as Chuck Berry (who also occupies an important place in the ongoing development of pop music), played PUNK ROCK. Likewise, the importance of the Sex Pistols as an inspiration to those working within the PUNK ROCK genre diminishes as we move away from this particular time and geographical location (i.e. London in 1977). Similarly, there are many groups who've worked within the genre who were never influenced or inspired by the Sex Pistols, most obviously those that were active prior to 1976.

V
WE NEED ANOTHER VIETNAM
American PUNK ROCK in the late seventies and the
economics of bootlegging

Obviously, there have been many different PUNK ROCK scenes in various geographical locations during the post-war period. However, few were as simultaneously focused and expansive as that to be found in Britain during the late seventies. It follows from this that we're unlikely to unearth such fine sources of contemporary compilation material as that discussed in the last chapter. Take, for example, the American garage rock scene(s) of the sixties. While much of this subgenre is now very well documented on various compilation series, such as *Nuggets* and *Pebbles*, these platters were put together many years after the tunes they feature were first issued. In the interest of brevity I will now move on from sixties garage rock by simply noting that it forms a major and integral segment of the PUNK ROCK genre. What I want to do instead is look at a broad section of the PUNK ROCK genre in the English speaking world from the late seventies onwards. As I have already pointed out, since PUNK ROCK as a genre has no fixed boundaries, it would be both pointless and counterproductive to attempt to be exhaustive in my treatment of the subject.

The bootleg compilation *Feel Lucky Punk?* has already been mentioned at the end of chapter one. This record is a fine sampler of archetypal late seventies style American and Australian punk rock, which brings together many of the best tracks to be found on the various volumes of the *Killed By Death* series. As was the case with the individual who issued the *Anarchy In The UK* CD, this is another bootlegger who is utterly shameless, and can't really be bothered to hide his identity. The gentleman in question is well known in the record trade for having put together the absolutely best series of sixties American garage rock compilations. Both the sleeve-notes, and the choice of Gonzo Hate Binge Records as a `cover' for this particular bootlegging operation are obvious clues to his identity. But as with our previous bootlegger, the owners of the copyright which is being infringed are unlikely to enjoy sufficient financial security to take legal action . and what's more, many of them have probably thanked him for reissuing their product!

Simply providing the track listing for *Feel Lucky Punk?* gives a good indication of the anti-social nature of sneering two-chord garage rock: Rocks – *Hanging On;* Queers – *I Don't Wanna Work;* Psycho Surgeons – *Horizontal Action;* Nervous Eaters – *Just Head;* News – *Tell Me Why;* Queers – *I'm Useless;* Violators – *N. Y. Ripper;* Hollywood Squares – *Hillside Strangler;* Lewd – *Kill Yourself;* Mad – *Disgusting;* Rocks – *Damn You;* Unnatural Axe – *They Saved Hitler's Brain;* Rocks – *Kick Her Out;* Queers – *At The Mall;* Nervous Eaters – *Get Stuffed;* Freestone – *Bummer Bitch;* Mad – *I Hate Music;* Nasal Boys – *Hot Love;* Queers – *This Place Sucks;* Leftovers – *I Only Panic When There's Nothing To Do;* Child Molesters – *Hillside Strangler;* Queers – *Kicked Out Of The Webelos.*

Yes, the principal concerns are sex, murder and other anti-social acts! In terms of lyrical content the Psycho Surgeons exhibit a typically Aussie PUNK facility for word play, rhyming as they do 'hospital traction' and 'horizontal action' in a speed freak hymn to lust. Likewise, the Nervous Eaters are distinctively American in their singer's up front statement of what's on his mind: 'Just head coz I'm in a rush / Just head that'll be enough.'

Although *Feel Lucky Punk?* is supposed to be a sampler of '77/'78 era PUNK ROCK, the Queers didn't issue their first record until 1982, and the four bootlegged tracks actually date from 1984, although they're wrongly attributed to 1983 on the sleeve of the Gonzo Hate Binge compilation. The bootlegger justifies the inclusion of the Queers on the grounds that their music hasn't been corrupted by 'shit hardcore' influences, and the band certainly don't appear out of place on the record. It was being bootlegged both here and on *Killed By Death* that transformed the Queers from complete unknowns into a cult among those who appreciate the joys of 'obscure' PUNK ROCK. This is a good example of bootlegging greatly benefiting the holders of an infringed copyright because in being bracketed with a clutch of collectable punk bands from an earlier period, the Queers were able to break through to an audience who liked their sound but was deeply suspicious of eighties exponents of the genre and related tendencies such as hardcore.

When the group's second album, *Love Songs For The Retarded,* appeared in 1993, every other record collector I encountered was asking, 'is that the same Queers who are on *Killed By Death* and *Feel Lucky Punk?*' There was a certain amount of confusion due to the band having parted company with the singer featured on their

1984 EP and the sound being somewhat smoother. Once it was confirmed that this was the same Queers, there was a steady demand for the group's deleted 1990 long player *Grow Up*, which was subsequently reissued. While all the band's output is energetic and tuneful, the more recent material lacks the hard-edged '77 style sound of early songs such as *We'd Have A Riot Doing Heroin* and *I Spent The Rent*. Like the previous two albums, the group's most recent release, *Beat Off*, features a Ramones influenced surf-punk sound, or put another way, it's perfect pop music for skateboarders and discerning record buyers of all ages.

The Child Molesters provide *Feel Lucky Punk?* with 'super-dumb sleaze-bag thud' in the shape of their first single, *Hillside Strangler*, which was both intentionally offensive and very badly recorded. Much of this cult group's output has appeared in recent years on the highly collectable Sympathy For The Record Industry label, some tracks being reissues while other work was previously unreleased. In a similar groove to *Hillside Strangler* is *(I Wanna See Some) Wholesale Murder*. However, the Child Molesters' greatest achievement was *13 Is My Lucky Number*, a masterpiece of 'bad taste' in which the band detail their liking for young girls, while simultaneously managing to rhyme 'jailbait' with 'statutory rape'.

It is worth remarking here that PUNK transgressions of 'good taste' are an important element of its antagonistic relationship towards the dominant culture. As Pierre Bourdieu points out in his book *Distinction: A Social Critique Of The Judgement Of Taste* (Routledge & Kegan Paul, London 1984), the notion of 'good taste' is culturally loaded. The 'anti-social' theatrics of PUNK ROCK are in many ways an attack on a key concept in the ideological armoury of 'serious culture'. Unfortunately, PUNK ROCK contestations of bourgeois aesthetics (whose entangled methodology seeks to justify social stratification on the basis of 'taste') are rarely articulated in anything other than, at best, a semi-conscious way. As a consequence, PUNK attacks on elitism can end up reinforcing the hegemonic position of the dominant culture, which knows very well how to defend itself against populism. Poorly articulated criticism can very easily be turned back against those antagonistic towards the reigning ideology of judgement and used as a justification for their continuing exclusion from the various institutions that simultaneously propagate and defend 'serious culture'. Intransigent exponents of 'bad taste' such as the Child Molesters, whose musical development underwent an unfortunate evolution in the direction of jazz, were probably more consciously aware of this state of affairs than other, less 'arty' 'PUNK ROCK' acts.

Another group who impinged on West Coast PUNK circles, and again had a heavily jazz influenced sound, were the Deadbeats. They recorded a Punk Rock classic in the form of *Kill The Hippies* and very little else, although their live set included songs such as *Hooked On Jailbait*. Like the Child Molesters, they appear to have had a conscious awareness of the subversive potential of 'anti-social' theatrics. While the Deadbeats and the Child Molesters currently enjoy cult status among record collectors, Burlesque (a British jazz rock band who also attempted to make inroads on the seventies PUNK circuit) remain well and truly forgotten. Again, as with the other jazz influenced bands under discussion, Burlesque possessed an awareness of the subversive potential of symbolic transgressions of 'good taste'. For example, the British band recorded a song in 1977 called *Steel Appeal* that detailed a pathological love affair between the singer and a wheelchair bound geriatric. The initial impact of all three of these jazz-'punk' groups was severely limited due to their adoption of a completely recuperated musical form. The cult status now enjoyed by the two American bands was initially derived from releases that conformed to the evolving PUNK ROCK format of the late seventies. It will be interesting to see if there is ever a Burlesque revival carried out on the back of the belated success the Deadbeats and the Child Molesters now enjoy among record collectors.

Moving on to yet another bootlegger, Dave Fergusson is so shameless that he not only puts his name on the illicit releases he issues as Destroy Tapes, he even includes his address. But then, as I've already pointed out, it's not as though he needs to lose sleep about infringing copyrights held by people who can't afford to enforce them. In his sleeve notes to the *What Stuff* compilation on Iloki, Chris Ashford who owns the rights to quite a number of 'obscure' late seventies PUNK ROCK recordings (he ran the Los Angeles based, and now legendary, independent What? Records label) concludes ruefully: 'I hope all you bootleggers out there might just give it up for a while and the rest of you... just enjoy it.'

However, Ashford must know that the small international band of obsessives bootlegging rare PUNK ROCK will continue illicitly reissuing these recordings regardless of his openly stated disapproval.

Most of them could make a bigger profit by pirating the likes of Dylan and Springsteen but avoid shit of this type because they are, first and foremost, music fans. Fergusson's operation is so low budget that there's clearly very little money involved, he is simply a long term Punk Rock psychotic who is, in any case, notorious for pissing away whatever money passes through his hands. It would be counter productive for even a large corporation to sue someone like Fergusson, he has no money and so it would be impossible to recover the costs of taking him to court.

Fergusson's *Hardcore History* runs to six C90 cassettes that retail for £2.50 each, and since the sales on individual volumes are probably struggling to reach the three figure mark, it doesn't take an accountant to work out that there's very little money involved. At the top end of this segment of the market, each volume of something like *Back To Front* sells a thousand copies on vinyl and a few thousand on CD. Of course, *Back To Front* is a completely legitimate operation which runs the following statement on its product:

> Thanks to all those people and labels which helped us with info and which gave the permission to put their material on this record. Some addresses have been dated, so we couldn't get in contact with all bands. Our challenge to these bands is: Get in touch with us!

Likewise, each volume of *Killed By Death* came out on vinyl in an edition of approximately 750 and these are now being reissued on CD in pressings of a few thousand. The history of this series is rather complex, because the name and concept created by the original bootlegger was bootlegged by two other individuals running their own pirate operations. The *Killed By Death* CD reissues are rumoured to emanate from yet another source which also deals legitimately in 'sixties-style' garage rock.

However, the small number of units sold in no way negates the importance of these compilations in defining and redefining the boundaries of the Punk Rock genre, in which there is, after all, a high premium placed on 'obscurity'. This is a very specialised segment of the record market, and although such modest sales would result in a considerable loss for a large corporation with high fixed costs, it is perfectly feasible for an independent operator to make modest profits on sales of just a few hundred units. Having said this, there are Punk Rock records, and bands, whose sales run into at least five, and possibly six, figures. Unlike much chart product, Punk Rock recordings may sell comparatively slowly but they do have a long shelf life, with successful titles still being re-pressed many years after they were first issued.

The British PUNK ROCK scene of the late seventies has become, at least among record collectors, a victim of its own success. English PUNK ROCK of the period has failed to appreciate in value precisely because of the comparatively high sales it enjoyed at that time, resulting in a glut of the product. Recently, the trend in high priced collectors items has been towards the rare European recordings of the late seventies and early eighties, made by bands who only began to penetrate the Anglo-American market posthumously. The prices paid for records by bands who were previously 'unknown' to PUNK ROCK collectors generally skyrockets after the group has been featured on a compilation series such as *Back To Front*. Within Europe, it is the Italian PUNK ROCK collectors who push up the prices, but what they are prepared to pay for obscure records pales in comparison to Japanese obsessives.

Fergusson's *Hardcore History* strays into the *Killed By Death* and *Back To Front* territory of genuine obscurities on volumes 4, 5 and 6, but the first three cassettes in the series feature American bands who will be familiar to anyone with more than a passing acquaintance with the PUNK ROCK genre. The Alley Cats, Avengers, Chain Gang, Crime, Dils, Electric Chairs, Germs, Misfits, Ramones, Randoms, Snatch, Venus And The Razorblades, Weirdos and the Zeros are among the groups featured on *Hardcore History 1*. Unfortunately, as the title of the series indicates, on later volumes Fergusson has a tendency to stray out of the PUNK ROCK genre and into the hardcore phenomenon.

While the *Hardcore History* series features material from the East Coast, the emphasis is very much on the West Coast, which is hardly surprising given that the most significant ideological Punk Rock scene in late seventies America developed in California. Rather unfortunately, the SF and LA scenes mutated into hardcore, something that Fergusson likes but which is of no interest to me. I will deal with the way the East Coast is represented on *Hardcore History* first, largely because there is not a great deal that needs to be said about it. Obviously, the Ramones' first four studio albums and the *It's Alive* recording of their New Year's Eve concert in Finsbury Park, occupy a place at the very centre of the PUNK ROCK genre. Songs such as *Teenage Lobotomy, Gimme Gimme Shock Treatment, Now I Wanna Sniff Some Glue, Cretin Hop* and *I Wanna Be Sedated* are classic examples of transgressive PUNK ROCK theatrics given a quasi-Baudrillardian spin. Clearly, one does not need to be acquainted with post-modern theory to appreciate what the Ramones were doing and it is hard to imagine even a 'contemporary cultural critic' taking these lyrics literally, although it would be a mistake to under-estimate the depths to which Groovy Greil Marcus can sink. Given that the present text is not concerned with the 'history' of specific bands, I can finish dealing with the Ramones by referring interested readers to Jim Bessman's book *The Ramones: An American Band* (St. Martin's Press, New York 1993) which is a typical example of the notoriously dull genre of pop music biography.

The only Electric Chairs track featured on *Hardcore History* is *Paranoia Paradise*. The band are crucial because singer Wayne County genuinely understood the subversive potential and transformative power of cultural transgression. County began his rock career as a transvestite, and continued it as a transsexual, allowing the public to witness his transformation from Wayne into Jayne. Between 1977 and the 1980 New Year's Eve live set *Rock 'N' Roll Resurrection*, the lyrical content of *Paranoia Paradise* mutated and the song was re-titled *Fucked By The Devil*. The live album captures County at her peak, simultaneously exploiting her transsexual status and the past history of the evolving PUNK ROCK genre by covering sixties garage rock classics such as *Are You A Boy?* The singer's transgressive humour is equally evident in original compositions such as *Mean Motherfuckin' Man, Fuck Off, Things Your Mother Never Told You, Cream In My Jeans, Bad In Bed* and *Toilet Love*. Interested readers should check out County's forthcoming autobiography *Man Enough To Be A Woman* (co-written with Rupert Smith, Serpent's Tail, London & New York 1995)

Fergusson doesn't bootleg the Dead Boys or the Dictators so, although each played an important role in the unfolding of the New York PUNK ROCK scene in the nineteen-seventies, I will not deal with them at this juncture. Initially, at least, participants in West Coast PUNK ROCK circles of the late seventies felt they were being overshadowed by events in London and New York. The frustration and sense of rivalry that arose from this situation is plainly evident on recordings such as *We Don't Need The English* by the Bags and *Let's Get Rid Of New York* by the Randoms, although this attitude was no doubt also fuelled by hostility felt towards individual British expatriates and East Coast 'Wasps' living in California. However, this West Coast 'particularism' was propagated in positive as well as negative forms, as can be seen from the song *Los Angeles* by X. It should go without saying that this antagonism was simply one side of a 'love-hate' relationship. British bands, in particular, were viewed as 'cool' by the very people who simultaneously disliked them for their comparative 'success'.

The West Coast scene contained many of the same elements that were prevalent in late seventies PUNK ROCK produced in other geographical locations. The Nuns, for example, had a fixation with theatrical nihilism which was revealed in songs such as *Decadent Jew, Savage, Suicide Child* and *Child Molester*. Prototypical PUNK ROCK sleaze-bag humour is equally evident in tunes such as *Killer Queers* by the Controllers, with its chorus of 'I need a blow job', and *Sit On My Face Stevie Nicks* by the Rotters which combines an attack on a 'boring old fart' with an upfront verbalisation of the singer's sexual desires:

> All night long I can't get no sleep / Don't know what to do without the taste of meat / It's that smell that gets me high / I love the feel of your upper thigh / So sit on my face / On my face / Sit on my face Stevie Nicks... When I first saw you I had a fit / Couldn't wait to eat your steamy clit / Think it's offensive well stick around / We'll make you puke and vomit like a hound...

Equally good are the very tuneful and genuinely 'extreme' Dils, whose first two singles *I Hate The Rich* and *Class War* were high points of late seventies Californian Punk Rock. However, it wasn't just the 'extremists' who released classic pop product; among the best of the West Coast bands of that period were a bunch of school-boys calling themselves the Zeros. Sometimes known among PUNK ROCK collectors as the Mexican Ramones, the Zeros recorded a handful of classic songs. Their first single *Wimp* is the best known of them, although later tunes such as *She's Just A Girl On The Block* demonstrate that the group maintained their ability to knock out poppy punk classics over the entire span of their five year career. One act who maintained a distance between themselves and the rest of the West Coast scene of that time were the legendary Crime. Hailing from San Francisco, the group are best known for their first single *Hot Wire My Heart*. They were also notorious for wearing police uniforms on stage and there is a hard to obtain but truly surreal video release of Crime performing at San Quentin jail in this garb to row upon row of seated prisoners.

Another of San Francisco's finest bands of the late seventies were the Avengers, whose melodic songs with titles like *I Believe In Me* and *White Nigger* placed them firmly within the subgenre of ideological Punk Rock. The lyrics to tunes such as *We Are The One* show very plainly the nebulous nature of punk 'politics' and make it clear that it is completely pointless to try and categorise these in terms of a left/right divide:

> We are the leaders of tomorrow / We are the ones to have fun / We want control, we want power / Not gonna stop until it comes / We are not Jesus Christ / We are not fascist pigs / We are not capitalists, industrialists / We are not communists / We are the one / We will build a better tomorrow / The youth of today will be the tool / America's children made for survival / Fate is our destiny and we shall rule / I am the one who brings you the power / I am the one who buries the past / A new species rise up from the ruin / I am the one that was made to last.

Among PUNK ROCK cognoscenti there is one West Coast band who, in terms of cult status, now stand head and shoulders above all their Hollywood rivals of the late seventies. They are the Germs. I do not want to give a detailed history of the Germs because something approximating that can be found in the booklet accompanying the posthumous *Cats Clause* ten inch album on the Munster label. Likewise, anyone interested in the wider West Coast scene of the late seventies is referred to *Hardcore California: A History Of Punk And New Wave* by Peter Belsito and Bob Davis (Last Gasp, San Francisco 1983). It has been suggested elsewhere that the Germs album *GI* was the first 'hardcore' record. Obviously, given my understanding of genre as something that is continuously evolving, and which consequently has flexible boundaries, I cannot concur with such a view. In any case, the Germs output sits more easily within the Punk Rock genre at its present stage of historical evolution than within the discourse known as hardcore.

In terms of PUNK ROCK aesthetics, the Germs most significant contribution to the genre is the auspiciously premature 1977 What? Records single *Forming*. On this the band clearly don't care whether or not they're ready to make a record, they are simply gonna do it anyway! The result is a brilliant example of raw and primitive Punk Rock that cuts through all the crap concerning professionalism that is put about by the corporate music establishment. As with most of the Germs product, it's the attitude that counts and this is considerably more impressive than the lyrics. It's the group's front that makes their music a quintessential example of ideological Punk Rock.

Exerting almost as seminal an influence as *Forming* on the ongoing development of the Punk Rock genre is/was *Germicide*, a live recording of the band's debut at the Whisky in LA which dates from June 1977. After introductions by Kim Fowley, Rodney Bingenheimer and Belinda Carlisle (who blurts 'the reason I'm not in the group anymore, because they're too dirty for me, they're sluts'), the Germs grind their way through *Forming, Sex Boy, Victim, Street Dreams, Let's Pretend, Get A Grip, Suicide Machine, Sugar Sugar, Teenage Clone* and *Grand Old Flag*, only just managing to hold the sound together. The complete 'incompetence' of the musicianship is both disarming and charming. During the cover of the Archies bubblegum classic *Sugar Sugar*, the Germs had instructed their friends to pelt them with food, and photographs of the performance show gunk dripping from the band. Three years later, singer Darby Crash transformed himself into a Punk Rock legend by overdosing on smack, an event that led fans to emblazon their leather jackets with the slogan 'THE GERMS WILL NEVER DIE'.

The fact that notorious music business hustler Kim Fowley promoted the Germs 'first' concert allows me to unite East and West Coast PUNK ROCK, while simultaneously returning to the issue of *Louie Louie* and the fact that Dave Marsh failed to deal with the majority of 'important' PUNK ROCK versions and variants of the tune in his book on the song. Fowley, known to fans as 'the Dorian Grey of rock 'n' roll', has been involved in pop music for a very long time and he pops up on the first volume of the garage rock series *Pebbles* with his hippie cash-in novelty item *The Trip*. Fowley also turns up on another sixties punk compilation series called *Girls In The Garage*, this time as Althea And The Memories doing a version of *Louie Louie* with new lyrics ('Do you think there's ever been a dance called the wheelchair / You do it sitting down...') that he's retitled *The Worst Record Ever Made*. Quasi-Sorelean notions of myth play a major role in the propagation of PUNK ROCK, and here's how the liner notes to *Girls In The Garage* describe the recording of *The Worst Record Ever Made*:

> The genius of Kim Fowley deserves greater recognition than we have room for here, but let's close with an incomparable example of his work from the Golden Age of record producing. Picture this scene:

Kim has rented a studio for an hour, filled it with session musician friends (probably all big names like Sandy Nelson, P.J. Proby, Mars Bonfire or Skip Batlyn) and sets them to jamming on the *Louie Louie* riff. Then, dashing into the street, he grabs some girls walking home from school, throws them into the studio, and tells them to sing backup, while he proceeds to improvise for two minutes. Then he realises the whole thing is out of control and tries to stop it, but nobody's listening to him. Released on Rubbish Records in 1966. Try to find it!

Now, while certain individuals have used Punk Rock as a springboard to pop stardom, genuine Punk Rock stars ought to be nothing less than born again losers. It should go without saying that genuine exponents of punk rock never become teen idols because even if they succeed in racking up a one hit wonder, mentally they never manage to leave the garage. One individual who, like Darby Crash of the Germs, epitomises the persona of the Punk Rock star is Stiv Bators. While Bators is best known for his work with the Dead Boys and the Lords Of The New Church, what must simultaneously be considered the high and low point of his career came when he was working as a solo 'artist', and it was Kim Fowley who instigated the incident that formed its basis. Forget about the Dead Boys arriving in New York from their native Cleveland to carve out a reputation as that absurd media creation 'the American Sex Pistols'. Jamie Reid and Johnny Rotten never wrote sneering punk lyrics along the lines of 'Look at me that way bitch / Your face is gonna get a punch' or 'Write on your face with my pretty knife / I wanna buy your precious life'. Nevertheless, the theatrical nihilism that typified much of Bators' career is inconsequential when compared to the fact that it was his destiny to remake *The Worst Record Ever Made*. Greg Shaw of Bomp Records tells the story in his sleeve notes to the posthumous *LA LA* CD of rare and unreleased Stiv Bators material:

> I still recall, vividly, the moment of frozen horror when Jim Mankey called sometime in the middle of the night to let me know that the studio where Stiv was supposed to be recording his new single had been invaded by a horde of refugees from Hollywood's closing hour, led by none other than Kim Fowley. I knew with a sinking feeling that they'd be there for hours, nothing useful would get done, and I'd have to pay the bills... On hand was an army of hangers on, including BeBe Buell, and various members of Sham 69 and the Runaways. Also along was Fowley protégé Tommy Rock, who helped

throw together the songs and arrangements that ended up being put on tape, instead of the planned single... *LA LA* rewrites *Louie Louie* as a kind of exegesis of Stiv's Hollywood experiences.

In other words, with a chorus of 'LA LA, I'm on a Hollywood high,' and a motley crew of backing singers, Fowley got Bators to re-record *The Worst Record Ever Made*. Add to that the fact that Bators went on to die in a hit and run accident and you have the stuff of PUNK legend.

Fowley, being a prototypical punk himself, had many other brushes with the genre during the seventies. The master's best shot at commercial success during this period was with the Runaways, a 'novelty' act consisting of five teenage girls. Songs such as *Cherry Bomb* and *Hollywood* are schlock classics, although the group is heard to best effect on the Marilyn CD *Born To Be Bad*, allegedly recorded five days after they'd been formed with Fowley getting it all down on a Roberts reel-to-reel tape recorder. Another Fowley creation, Venus And The Razorblades, turn up on *Hardcore History 1* with the tracks *I Wanna Be Where The Boys Are* and *Punk-A-Rama*. Fowley's 'there are no depths to which I cannot sink' attitude makes Malcolm McLaren look like a provincial bore.

Before abandoning, for the time being, the subject of American PUNK ROCK, I want to reiterate that to some degree my starting point is arbitrary. It should be clear from the preceding pages that it would have been just as useful to focus on sixties garage rock, of which there are scores of compilations to assist in a delineation of that particular PUNK ROCK subgenre. Alternatively, I could have begun in the eighties with the Mystic Records series *Sound Of USA Cities*. The first Mystic Records volume is dedicated to Washington DC and the track listing features many archetypal aspects of the PUNK ROCK genre: Motor Morons – *Too Many Girls;* Phlegm – *Charlie's Secret;* The Thing That Wouldn't Leave – *King Kong Bundy;* The Platinum Slugs – *Easy Mark;* Receptacles – *No;* Bad Vibes – *No One Knows Who They Are Or Where They Come From;* Asbestos Rockpyle – *Captain Blue;* Roadside Pets – *Inside You;* Sybil – *I Am TV;* Madhouse – *Wardrobe;* Painkillers – *I'm Living On Bulk Food;* Pure Evil – *Frustration;* Christian Nightmare – *Hate;* Sarcastic Orgasm – *Forum Letter.*

The point I am making is that to understand this genre we have to immerse ourselves in its musical products and once we are orientated within the tradition it becomes easier to make sense of its shifting boundaries. I've already said that it's not only pointless, but counterproductive, to attempt to produce a definitive account of the subject due to its flexible parameters. I have no intention of utilising the list as an organising principle within this text and many PUNK ROCK records that are personal favourites of mine remain uncited. Nevertheless, it is necessary to cover a broad range of material, most of which is not going to be treated in any depth, because rather than wasting my time with either a populist chronicle of a given style of music or an abstract account of the genesis of cultural formations per se, I am providing a concrete description of one particular musical genre.

VI

DESCENT INTO THE MAELSTROM
British PUNK ROCK 1978 to 1980

B ritain in 1977 provided the spatial location for a crucial
turning point in the existence of ideological Punk Rock. There
is no real sense of 'ideological' development (or degeneration if
you conceptualise change as being essentially negative) between
the rhetoric used by Punk Rock bands such as the Fugs in the mid-
sixties, and later examples of the genre, for example the Deviants
or the MC5. It was only with the new wave explosion of 1977 that
it became possible to transform quantity into quality. However, before dealing with the four stage unfolding of Punk Rock between
1977 and the mid-nineties, I wish to look at some dead ends as far
as this particular genre is concerned, while simultaneously stress-
ing that this does not necessarily imply that they were unproduc-
tive in terms of new, or at any rate other, cultural discourses.

Various stabs have been made at parodying ideological Punk
Rock but without doubt the *Snuff Rock* EP by Alberto Y Los Trios
Paranoias, released on Stiff Records in September 1977, was simultaneously one of the best and most ill-judged homages to the
subgenre. The record was such a perfect imitation of its intended
target that it failed to work as parody and became instead a great
Punk Rock novelty item. Punk Rock ideology isn't coherent in its
rhetorical posturing and so the lyrics to *Kill* simply blend into the
discourse: 'I don't give a damn / I don't fuckin' care / Gonna kill
me mum and dada / And pull out me hair / I'm fed up with the
dole and the human race / I'm gonna cut me liver out and shove it
in your face / Kill, yeah kill!' These and the words to the other
three tracks moronically reiterate Punk Rock platitudes, which were
never intended as anything other than rhetoric in the first place.
For example, *Gobbing On Life*, which is every bit as good as *Kill*,
includes lines such as 'Living isn't easy when you're young and
broke and on the dole' and 'Living is a cliché it's all been done
before / Death is the only thing we've got left to live for.'

A less self-conscious exploration of the entangled subgenres of
punk rock and Punk Rock can be found on the Depressions' epony-
mous first album released by Barn Records in 1978. The platter
opens with the classic *Screw Ya*:

> There's a certain little number gonna make it with / And she's stand-
> ing at the back of the hall / I know she's a raver all my mates have
> laid her behind the classroom wall / I can't wait for the bell to ring
> to show her how I use my tool / Tonight I'm gonna screw ya... Let's
> go down to the woods where I can feel your goods / I want to know
> where my mates have been / Better be no lies about you parting
> your thighs because I've heard you can be quite obscene / Slip you
> hand down there let me undo you jeans / Let me give it to you really
> mean / Tonight I'm gonna screw ya... gonna give it to you so hard
> that you won't forget / Bring tears to your eyes and cream to your
> thighs / I'm the best thing that you've had so far yet...

If this sounds like 'socialism of the trenches' and to a certain
degree it does, then the sheer incoherence of the 'messages' given
off by the entire album demonstrate that such rhetoric shouldn't
be taken too seriously; in the end it is simply brilliantly empty
'teenage' posturing. In *Chains And Leather*, the singer howls that his
girlfriend treats him 'like a dog', while *Career Girl* unintentionally
demonstrates the complexity of social stratification. Without wishing to deny the existence of patriarchy, it should be obvious that
class is an equally important factor mediating the distribution of
social power, as is evident from the sorry saga narrated by the Depressions:

> She's studying her books / She's left me in the cold / She's gonna be
> a teacher just you wait and see / And now I'm on the dole queue
> she's got no time for me / There's nothing really like her on this side
> of town / I won't see my career girl / She's just not around...

The Depressions are what the Stranglers would have been if they'd
belonged on the PUNK ROCK scene, instead of being a bunch of
bores. The consciously adopted and very coherent ideology of mi-
sogyny spouted by the Stranglers is utterly tedious. For examples
of this see the chapter on the band in Caroline Coon's *1988: The
New Wave Punk Rock Explosion* (Second edition, Omnibus Press, London 1982). While one can argue the toss about whether or not the
Depressions were 'sexist' and to be honest I don't really care, there
can be no doubt that the Stranglers were self-professed male su-
premacists. Apart from ideological coherence, the other important
difference between the two groups is that of sound; while keyboard
playing is an important feature of the Stranglers music, the Depressions were a guitar based band. Even on their second album, *If
You Know What I Mean*, when the Depressions were evolving away
from PUNK ROCK towards a more 'mainstream' rock sound (and had

71

shortened their name to the DPs as a way of signifying this), their music was infinitely superior to that of the Stranglers. Although by 1979 the Depressions had disappeared without trace, having spent their record company advances on drugs and a huge truck, they remain one of the best bands to have come out of Brighton, beating the Levellers hands down any day!

Another PUNK ROCK band who disappeared, albeit in a far more spectacular way, were Adam And The Ants. Although the group later split asunder, creating two of the great pop groups of the nineteen-eighties (Bow Wow Wow and a combo who retained the original name), from 1977 through to the following year, the Ants attempted to push ideological Punk Rock in one very particular direction. The slogan 'Ant Music For Sex People' summarises this highly entertaining evolutionary dead end for the Punk Rock subgenre. In their early days, the band kicked off their set with *Plastic Surgery*, a hilarious song which included these lines of advice to a car crash victim whose face has been 'restored': 'Don't go sitting in the sun / Your new face might start to run / Just forget your make-up scheme / Clean your face with Mr Sheen.'

The Ants had a twisted sense of humour, hence their black leather stage wear and songs about perversion. Typical of their 'high' kitsch stance was *Whip In My Valise*, with its chorus of 'Your sadistic suits my masochistic / There's a whip in my valise / Who taught you to torture'. Even better is *Beat My Guest*, which wasn't issued on vinyl until 1981, when it was placed on the B-side of kiddie pop hit *Stand And Deliver*. Who knows what ten year old Adam Ant fans made of the lyrics:

> Tie me up and hit me with a stick / Beat me, beat me / Use a truncheon or a household brick / Beat me, beat me / Black and blue, baby I love you... Hit me please make me bleed... There's so much happiness behind my tears / Beat me, beat me / I pray you beat me for ten thousand years / Beat me, beat me...

Unfortunately, very few of the songs the Ants played live prior to their vinyl debut have been officially released and even those that made it onto the B-sides of their early eighties pop hits featured fresh arrangements that lost in impact what they'd gained in sophistication. Numbers such as *Fat Fun*, which are only available on bootlegs, provide a fine metaphorical account of the twisted love-hate relationship that exists between Punk Rock idols and their audience:

Baby you're so overweight / Baby you're no one / Baby you're an ugly date / Looking for someone / So crave on fat fun, yeah / Fat fun / You look like a fucking walrus / Laying on the beach / You're too fat to see yourself / You're just my porky peach / So crave on fat fun, yeah / Fat fun / One day girl I'm gonna take you out / I'm gonna stop your meals / Baby I'll sew up your mouth / Till your stomach squeals / So crave on fat fun, yeah / Fat fun!

What makes the Ants in particular, and Punk Rock in general, so appealing is that it doesn't care if it offends. Take, for example, the words to *It Doesn't Matter*: 'I'd love to kiss you baby / Fall for your charms / But that's all over when you lift up your arms / It doesn't matter / It doesn't matter / I'll get by with another, baby you smell.' Given that during the late seventies the Ants had a mixed race drummer, kids at their gigs were unlikely to miss the point that the song *Puerto-Rican* was intended as an attack on racism. As a result, Adam Ant's lyrical approach to this subject was typically taboo breaking, he simply confronted his audience with bigotry and hate:

A chick like you is oh so rare / You get off on his greasy hair / You've got a smart apartment / You've got central heating / Why go and waste it on a Puerto-Rican / I'm gonna light up a beacon on a Puerto-Rican / Strike a matchstick on his head / Light up a beacon on a Puerto-Rican / Watch me smile as he drops down dead.

Unfortunately, with the passing years the irony in these words is much less apparent than it would have been in 1978. Although the Ants used *Dirk Wears White Sox* as the title of their first album, they never officially issued the song of the same name. This is a shame because it gave Mel Brooks circa *The Producers* a run for his money:

If you have a social problem / Prospects of success are slim / We just hope that you will telephone / Say 'Hello is Heinrich in?' / We will send our representatives / Don't be frightened when they call around / For they are all men of action / They will kick your front door down / You've got to concentrate on kicks / In a concentration camp / Off with the bloody dicks / In a concentration camp / We get rid of foolish people / Brothers, sisters, cousins on... Come along we'll be delighted / You can get a uniform for free / Shiny boots of soft black leather / Oh how proud your mum would be / You've got to concentrate on kicks / In a concentration camp / Off with their bloody dicks / In a concentration camp / Do what you wanna do / See what you wanna see / Lock them up in a prison / Throw the key away / Now the ones who laugh at you / Thought you were a clown / Gamble fate against your hate / Falling on the ground / We'll go to a Berlin nightclub / All the acts are so risqué / Many people have a

motto / Boy tomorrow, girl today / Now's the time to leave you
wardrobe / Just forget your social bent / Bring it all out in the open /
We can use your decadence...

While these words are anything but profound, it's worth quoting
them at length because they are both very funny and typical of
taboo breaking Punk Rock lyrics during the late seventies. They
also illustrate that rather than being socially progressive, Punk Rock
contained a provocative ambiguity.

After dealing with PUNK music in the first chapter, I have subsequently concentrated on lyrics because these have provided a focus
in the work of 'contemporary cultural critics' and other cretins who
are idiotic enough to look for 'the meaning of life' in plastic platters. However, the music should not be overlooked since it is as
much a vehicle for the 'nuances' of the genre as the words. Likewise, the 'beat' is a means of whipping the listener into a state of
excitement, which in its turn makes them more receptive to the
lyrics, regardless of their content. To a large extent PUNK ROCK
depends on volume for its impact, and the thumping great rhythm
literally affects the muscular structure of the body.

As a genre, PUNK ROCK is to a large degree shaped by the response of an international audience to what, perhaps, appears to
be an unending stream of records. Nevertheless, live performance
occupies a peculiarly important position among exponents of this
style of music. Although in my teenage years I attended concerts
by a good many of the bands who have been cited on previous
pages, this is not of sufficient interest to warrant detailed description. Instead, I will restrict myself to a series of anecdotes concerning one particular group, in the hope that this will give a flavour of
what it was like to follow any number of bands.

Although I'd run into Frazer Towman, the first Crisis singer, at
various PUNK ROCK gigs in 1977, I missed the band's first few public
appearances out of sheer laziness. I finally caught them live at
their fifth gig in January 1978. I can remember walking into Woking
town centre and a couple of kids of fifteen, my age at the time,
trying to pick a fight. The lippier of the two bastards attempted to
come on all theatrical, slowly removing his leather gloves. He didn't
like Punks, although seeing as I was dressed in a sixties tonic jacket,
shirt, Levis and boots, with very short hair, I'd located myself somewhere between Punk and the re-emerging Mod and Skinhead sub-
cultures. Anyway, when I gave the more aggressive bozo a hard

shove into the on-coming traffic, these two idiots realised that despite being alone, I wasn't going to be pushed around, so they pissed off. In 1977, and at the beginning of '78, most 'PUNK violence' occurred outside concert halls, but over the next couple of years things started getting a lot more fraught at 'new wave' gigs.

I got down to the Centre Halls and there was a real buzz because Menace and Sham 69 were top of the bill. I hadn't been inside long when Crisis came on. I wasn't too impressed by the drummer, Insect Robin Ledger aka the Cleaner, who looked like a twat thanks to his beard. However, once the band struck up, Frazer leapt on stage dressed in rubber trousers and a rapist's mask and I was well impressed. The songs were basic PUNK ROCK thrash with polemical lyrics: 'I am a militant / I am a picket / I fought at Lewisham / I fought at Grunwick / See, see the lies / See the lies civilise me / See, see the lies / See the lies can't you see?' or 'Search and destroy / Search and destroy the Nazis / The National Front / Smash the National Front / Annihilate, annihilate, annihilate, annihilate, annihilate'. Of course, it turned out that the words were written by rhythm guitarist Doug P. (who was in the International Marxist Group) and bassist Tony Wakeford (who was a member of the Socialist Workers Party). The cream on the cake was lead guitarist Lester Jones, aka Lester Picket, who could not only play very well, he also did an excellent impression of Mick Jones taking off Keith Richards.

It didn't take a 'genius' to work out Crisis had been inspired by the Clash, but what was interesting was that songwriters Doug and Tony took Strummer's revolutionary rhetoric seriously. Although the dialectical evolution of Punk Rock was to progress in a diametrically opposed direction from that in which Crisis were attempting to push it, the group nevertheless had an intuitive grasp of what the genre was about. Before playing a key role in the promotion of the Oi! movement, future *Sun* hack Gary Bushell hyped Crisis as reminding him 'of Sham a couple of months back, musically simple and muscular' (*Sounds* 16 September 1978) and 'a clenched fist rammed hard into the flabby belly of the just-for-fun music punk has become' (*Music To March To, Sounds* 18 November 1978). Bushell understood that the way forward for ideological Punk Rock was to rhetorically take to the streets. Crisis appeared to be doing just that, although the fact that at least some of the band took their 'revolutionary communist' image seriously prevented them emulating Sham 69's chart success.

When I think of Crisis all sorts of images flash through my mind. I can remember a whole bunch of the band's friends stealing crates of lager from behind the bar when the group played South Bank Polytechnic. Then there was the time in Brixton when Ken, the Skinhead junkie, jumped on stage to wave a knife about and threaten to cut up the bastard who'd punched out his girlfriend. She'd actually passed out from alcoholic excess. Another time, Rockin' Pete, a Teddy Boy, turned up at a Hackney gig to announce that he'd finally joined the Socialist Workers Party as though this was an act of some great significance! Then there was the performance on a side-stage at the second Anti-Nazi League Carnival when guitarist Doug P. was carted off to hospital after being electrocuted. But what I remember mainly were punch-ups, towards the end of the band's brief life it seemed as though there were always fights at Crisis gigs.

The most famous Crisis ruck was rather inaccurately reported under the headline *Rudies Don't Care* (*Sounds* 7 July 1979). An equally distorted account of the night can be found in the pro-situ pamphlet *Like A Summer With A Thousand Julys* by ex-King Mob members Dave and Stuart Wise, whose even sillier text *The End Of Music* did a great deal to help promote the ludicrous notion that PUNK ROCK was somehow 'musical Situationism'. The actual cause of this particular 'punk riot' was not, as the 'Wise' brothers falsely claim, various Boot Boys being refused entry to the Acklam Hall in Notting Hill, but a Ladbroke Grove Skin who'd been granted admission, attempting to feel up a girl who followed Crisis. Taking exception to this, the chick booted the bastard in the bollocks, severely crippling the cunt. The slime-bag was too embarrassed to admit to his mates that he'd been beaten up by a bird and so he pointed me out as the person who'd given him the kicking.

I was standing in front of the stage as Crisis played, surrounded by mates, but the Ladbroke Grove Skins wrongly assumed I was on my own. When four of these twats attempted to kick my head in, they quickly found the odds turning against them as not only the audience but also the band, who'd leapt off-stage, waded in on my side. The Ladbroke Grove Skins were lucky to escape from the hall without any particularly grievous injuries. Crisis finished their set and a reggae band was playing when the Skins returned mob handed, they'd rounded up sixty mates who were tooled up with hammers and pick-axe handles. This crew attempted to charge the security on the door but quick thinking Crisis fans formed a defensive line and beat them back. Meanwhile, the reggae band had locked themselves and their gear in a back room. Simultaneously, the Crisis crew threw a barricade of tables and chairs against the door while piping was ripped from the walls for use as offensive weapons.

Never inclined to stick to defensive tactics and having secured the hall assorted members of Crisis and their hardcore following stormed out into the street to lay into the mob besieging the venue. Among the more memorable of improvised weapons were motorcycle helmets that were brought cracking down onto cropped scalps. With numerous injuries on both sides, the Ladbroke Grove Skins were eventually beaten off by the superior fighting skills of Crisis and their friends. Although the band's transit had been trashed, with all windows smashed, the motor started and the crew loaded up the gear before piling in. Everyone thought the first stop was going to be Brixton but just down the road we spotted two of the Boot Boys who'd started the trouble in the hall. The driver pulled up and a score of Skinheads and punks leapt from the van.

The two Ladbroke Grove Skins ran into the very hospital where those injured during the ruck had been taken for treatment. One was caught and given a kicking in front of a night nurse; the bozo had landed in the right place to have his wounds stitched up, perhaps he knew that he'd never evade his pursuers as he legged it into casualty. The other Skin disappeared down a maze of corridors and, as far as I'm concerned, has never been heard of again. It should be made clear that this wasn't punk versus Skinhead violence, which was very common at the time. Although the majority of people associated with Crisis could be loosely described as 'punks', bassist Tony Wakeford had adopted the Skinhead look before this incident, as had some of those who followed the band. Likewise, a segment of the audience attending Crisis gigs were by this time geared up in rockabilly threads. The ability of this subculturally mixed crew to see off the Ladbroke Grove Skins contrasts very favourably with the next occasion on which these Boot Boys besieged the Acklam Hall. Incapable of fighting their way out, Oi! band the Last Resort and their fans, who at the time were being portrayed by the media as the ultimate violent hooligans, had to be rescued by the police!

Other incidents I can relate about Crisis are much funnier. For example, having gone through a succession of stickmen, Crisis recruited Luke Rendall as their new drummer. Rendall was very nervous about his debut with the band, needlessly so because he was a great musician, as he demonstrated both that night and on many other occasions with Crisis and Theatre Of Hate. To psyche himself up, Luke gulped down a handful of blues and because he was speeding he played the songs far faster than usual. Two numbers into the set, rhythm guitarist Doug P. turned around and asked Rendall if he could slow down. The drummer shock his head and spat 'no, mate, no,' before launching into the next song at double speed.

One gig in Reading ran so late that after staying for the encores, the hardcore following missed the last train home. Crisis got about in a small bakery van but nevertheless felt obliged to provide transport for their mates. That night there were four people crammed onto a front seat that was designed for two passengers. So that everyone else could fit in the back, kids had to lie on top of both the equipment and each other. Coming out of Reading, the transit was stopped by some cops who'd observed that the vehicle was severely overloaded. The filth told everyone to get out and couldn't believe their eyes when fifteen youths emerged from the rear of the van. 'Jesus!' a boneheaded constable exclaimed, 'we've enough of 'em 'ere for an identification parade!'

A more typical anecdote about Crisis concerns their reputation as violent nutters. Certain members of the group and some of their followers liked fighting. Whenever the opportunity arose, they'd beat up neo-fascists, and if there weren't any Nazis about to give a kicking, they'd pick on anyone, including each other. The group's last gig was as support act to Magazine at Surrey University in May 1980. While the gear was being set up, a friend of the band called Aggy threw food over Dexter No-Name, who at that time handled vocals for Crisis. Dexter was less than pleased and proceeded to hospitalise his mate. The Student Entertainment Officer was totally freaked out, and ran off screaming: 'the gig hasn't even started and already you're beating each other up!'

Crisis are at once typical and atypical of late seventies ideological Punk Rock at the cross-roads of dialectical change. The revolutionary commitment of Doug and Tony was at odds with the attitude of the rest of the band and their fans, most of whom weren't interested in taking politics very seriously. The band issued two singles and a mini-album during their brief career, while one single appeared posthumously. They played something approaching a hundred gigs in Britain, mainly political benefits, and did a Rock Against Racism tour of Norway. While I went to a lot of gigs in the late seventies, I saw Crisis more times than any other band and so it is only natural for me to use them as a means of illustrating the type of activity that will reinforce the image of any given group as an ideological Punk Rock combo. Obviously, image cannot be reduced to behaviour but, alongside clothes and record sleeves, it plays a major role in how any given group is perceived by the public.

Crisis adopted a *modus operandi* that could be characterised as underground, after unfortunate experiences with a couple of independent labels they proceeded to put out their own product. This is a mark of their deviation from the rhetoric of Punk Rock and the beginnings of a tentative engagement with other forms of activity in which such ideals move out of the symbolic realm and take on a material reality. Some of these proclivities found a more conscious articulation in Death In June, the band founded by Doug P. and Tony Wakeford after Crisis split. However, this is not the place to deal with such issues. In all probability, theoretical work in this area will be left to less capable hands because I have no plans to compose a text about those tendencies whose activities were simultaneously related and opposed to the rhetoric of 'ideological' Punk Rock. The point to remember here is that Crisis were considerably more successful than the average band issuing their own records in 1979/80. If Crisis had been a typical Punk Rock band, they would have signed to an independent label who would have provided them with greater sales and a smaller percentage of revenue from their record releases.

In fact, most bands assumed that their career trajectory would take a sudden leap once they'd signed a deal with a major label. However, the corporate music industry is just as likely to be a highway to oblivion as a ticket to success. A typical example of this process is provided by Masterswitch, who I saw on the bill alongside Sham, Menace, Speedometers and Crisis at Woking Centre Halls in January 1978. Masterswitch were a bunch of poseurs and to wind them up, I leapt on stage with two other punks, before proceeding to scream into a microphone set up for backing vocals. The group were well pissed off and stormed off stage, where they called upon Jimmy Pursey of Sham 69 to restore order. Masterswitch then played a few more numbers after which the singer shouted 'see you at Wembley' before disappearing into a dressing room. A few months later their only single, *Action Replay*, came out on the CBS subsidiary Epic. Instead of becoming a stadium act, the group sank so completely without trace that I've yet to meet a record dealer specialising in late seventies new wave and PUNK ROCK who has heard of them, let alone is capable of naming this release.

Another PUNK ROCK group who signed to a major label and yet failed to make much of an impact were London. Their MCA long player, *Animal Games*, is much better than the more collectable Sub-urban Studs album *Slam*, on the quasi-independent Pogo label. Nevertheless, it's *Slam* that's been reissued on CD in the Anagram *Punk Collectors Series*. No doubt this is partly because it's generally easier to licence product that was independently released, although it also reflects the way in which a certain type of record collector has bought into a highly nebulous notion of 'independence'. Of course, it is only fair to admit that London didn't impress me when I caught them live in May 1977, but then it may have been a duff gig. In retrospect, drummer John Moss is both an asset and a li-ability. I was impressed by Moss when I caught him beating time with the Damned in December 1977, in what turned out to be a very temporary replacement of Rat Scabies. However, many PUNK ROCK record collectors will be put off London by the fact that Moss went on to achieve fame as the drummer with chart topping Culture Club.

Northerners Cyanide also signed to a major label, but went no-where fast despite making all the noises Pye Records expected from a PUNK ROCK band. *Hate The State* and *Mac The Flash* on the group's self-titled debut album feature plenty of rhetorical transgression. The group's third and last single recently turned up on *Back To Front Volume 5* and this will no doubt lead to a revival of interest in the band. While Cyanide went nowhere, Dead Fingers Talk were going backwards, since they sounded like an English version of Television on their Pye long player *Storm The Reality Studios*. Only

We Got The Message came anywhere close to the PUNK ROCK genre and songs like *Nobody Loves You When You're Old And Gay* showed that their interests really lay elsewhere. Polydor did much better with the Jam but failed to capitalise on their Glasgow based 'mod' signing the Jolt, whose songs epitomised the late seventies punk rock lyrical approach with titles such as *I Can't Wait* and *No Excuses*.

In terms of kitsch, Raped, who recorded on the independent Parole label, took Punk Rock to a logical dead end. Their brand of Glam Punk tended towards transvestism and the band demonstrated that nothing was beneath them by calling their first EP *Pretty Paedophiles*. In dealing with this group, whose image was a good deal more significant than their music, I can best illustrate their impact by relating an anecdote about purchasing their product. There is a record dealer in Worthing who is notorious for his right-wing views and the fact that he was once a member of the National Front, as I discovered from several South Coast acquaintances after relating how excited he'd become when I'd purchased secondhand Skrewdriver platters from his shop. Since this creature had provided replacement copies of numerous PUNK records I'd long ago lost, I went back a month or so later, where among other things I picked up the Raped single *Cheap Night Out*. The best thing about this record is its tacky picture sleeve, and it was worth a lot more than the pound I paid to see the look on the right-armed record dealer's face when he rung up the item and it dawned on him that rather than being a 'patriot', I was actually some kind of 'pervert'. The bozo was seriously distressed! This is, of course, what PUNK ROCK is all about. As well as creating an imagined community, it brings into being enemies who are disgusted by everything the genre represents.

VII
BACK STREET KIDS
Oi! and the unfolding of the Punk Rock dialectic

By 1980, it was obvious to music journalist Gary Bushell that because Oi! did not yet exist, it was necessary to invent it. To qualitatively transform Punk Rock, bands such as Sham 69, Menace and the Cockney Rejects had quantitatively increased the level of rhetoric about being working class until they brought about a major mutation within the subgenre. When Sham 69 sang 'I don't need no flash car to get me around / I can take the bus to the other side of town' in *Hey Little Rich Boy*, they were aiming at an even lower common denominator than the Clash on the potentially incendiary *White Riot*. If the arrival of late seventies ideological Punk Rock had been announced by a Star in the West (despite rehearsing in North London, the Clash promoted their music as the 'sound of the Westway' and their first album featured a picture of rioting in Notting Hill Gate), then the resurrection of this subgenre as Oi! took place in the proletarian East (End).

It should go without saying that as a subgenre of ideological Punk Rock, Oi! has no fixed point of origin. Many bands now considered a part of the Oi! canon were recording long before the term had been invented. *Oi! The Album* features a number of bands who, at least initially, were known as New Punk, for example the Cockney Rejects, Peter And The Test Tube Babies and the Exploited. Other bands included on this sampler, for instance the Angelic Upstarts and Slaughter And The Dogs, are difficult to reconcile with the Oi! label because their initial success dates from the British PUNK ROCK explosion of the late seventies which preceded the New Punk phenomena, and the latter band simply don't sound rough enough to merit the 'street rock' description. Likewise, another Oi! favourite, Cock Sparrer, are hard to fit into any notion of PUNK ROCK whatsoever, their arrangements and playing are too articulate and too close to mainstream rock to sit easily within the genre. It was their lyrics and image that retrospectively earned them the PUNK ROCK and Oi! labels.

Obviously, the genesis of any genre or subgenre is going to be confused. Different things are thrown together in an attempt to create a fresh cultural formation but much of what is initially associated with the new term is abandoned as the canon evolves over time and simultaneously sinks its roots deeper and deeper into the past. While there were various 'revival' movements in the wake of the British PUNK ROCK explosion of the late seventies, the majority of these failed to bear fruit of any significance because they were unable to bring together elements that, at least initially, appeared to be fantastically antagonistic towards each other. The Mod revival, for instance, produced a handful of great records, the output of the Purple Hearts immediately springs to mind, but since it simply went back to the influence of the Who and Small Faces on late seventies PUNK ROCK and added a bit of amphetamine frenzy to that sound, it was incapable of producing anything of great novelty. There was more mileage in the ska revival which combined the musical muscle of the 'new wave' explosion with Jamaican sounds of the mid-sixties, but since there had already been much talk of a PUNK/reggae crossover, the results were not as surprising as they might otherwise have appeared.

The original Skinhead movement had not produced a music of its own, although it was happy to dance to Tamla Motown and early reggae. Thus the combination of Skinhead fashion and PUNK music was at first quite a novelty, although it was natural enough that those ideological Punks who were looking for a sartorial rhetoric to emphasise their theatrical immersion in the working class would gravitate towards this look, which was perceived as being uncorrupted by 'middle class' influences. I do not wish to suggest here that there were no middle class Skinheads. Even if they happened to be downwardly mobile, a small percentage of Boot Boys enjoyed privileged upbringings. Although, at least until recently in the UK, the bulk of youths adhering to the cult have come from working and lower middle class backgrounds, there are notable exceptions. For example, 'Nazi Chris Henderson', singer with the band Combat 84, admittedly more of a Bonehead than a Skinhead, was educated at the exclusive Charterhouse school.

The only Skinhead band to make it from *Oi! The Album* onto the follow up *Strength Thru Oi!* were the 4 Skins. Both of this band's contributions to the first Oi! album are certified rhetorical Punk Rock classics, *Wonderful World* was typically sarcastic, while *Chaos* featured the deadpan delivery of lyrics such as 'people that we don't beat up we're gonna fucking shoot.' The band's contributions to *Strength Thru Oi!* were *1984* and *Sorry* which are good but not brilliant. Nevertheless, the group quickly established their output as central to the Oi! genre. Their cynical 'street' humour is evident in both the name 4 Skins, not the most subtle of puns, and the words to songs like *Clockwork Skinhead*:

> Wearing braces and red, white and blue / Doing what he thinks he ought to do / Used to be a punk and a Mod too / But it's just a phase he's going through / He's a clockwork Skinhead / Just a clockwork Skinhead / Clockwork Skinhead / Got no choice / Clockwork Skinhead / Just a clockwork Skinhead / Clockwork Skinhead / One of the boys / Take him in a pub buy him a beer / Tell him what he wants to hear / Wind him up like a clockwork toy / Wants to be a man but he's just a boy / He's a clockwork Skinhead... Believes everything the papers say / What's he gonna be today / What is it, it to be / Will he be himself or will he copy me? / He's a clockwork Skinhead...

The other notable contributors to *Strength Thru Oi!* are the Last Resort, with the tracks *Working Class Kids* and *Johnny Barden*. The latter song is about a friend of the band banged up for killing a bloke who offered him a place to stay and then wanted to have sex with the kid. The lyrics are uncharacteristically coy, avoiding the obvious rhyme in the chorus when the group sing 'Killed his fear / When he killed the man.' Obviously sensitive to the possibility that they might be accused of being 'right-wing', the band also changed the title of one of their songs from *Stormtroopers In Sta-Press* to the tautologically more satisfying *Skinheads In Sta-Press*. Lyrically, the group are heard to best effect on numbers such as *Soul Boys*:

> Out they go wearing baggy slacks / Shiny shoes, flasher Macs / The way they dance makes me sick / They don't half look like a bunch of pricks / Soul Boys with Hawaiian shirts / On the lookout for teenage flirts / Did you get it? / Did you score? / Did you fuck the little whore? / I don't care, no not a bit / I don't give a fucking shit / About you... Soul Boys are a bunch of cunts / They're just a load of fucking runts / They can't fight, they can't scrap / All they do is run, run, run, run / Soul Boys in Hawaiian shirts... with pointy shoes and purple hair / Go to a disco stand and stare / When you get there you stand and pose / What you need is a punch on the nose...

If I have quoted these lyrics at length it is precisely because this is necessary to illustrate the nature of Oi!'s street level posturing. In qualitatively transforming Punk Rock by quantitatively increasing the amount of self-conscious rhetoric based on socially constructed notions of what it is to be working class, Oi! bands were protecting their music from arty farty trendies such as Groovy Greil

Marcus, who might otherwise have attempted to appropriate and deform it as something that could be incorporated into high cultural discourse. Of course, the fact that Marcus is repelled by Oi! is simply a mark of his lack of intellectual sophistication, since its very theatricality and deliberately crude articulation make this particular subgenre an easy target for any individual who has mastered the necessary codes and wishes to present themselves as operating at the cutting edge of 'serious culture'. Oi!'s transgressive qualities, particularly its alleged 'sexism' and 'nationalism', are its sole protection against such a calamity. These qualities are seen as being in very poor 'taste' by those 'middle class' bureaucrats who are very adept at fucking people over but dislike social antagonisms interfering with their oppressive administrative practices.

However, to move from this to the conclusion that all Oi! is 'rightwing' or even 'fascist' is absurd, as I will show by examining the output of two 'leftist' Oi! groups, the Oppressed and the Blaggers. We can in any case be certain that 'street rock' is not in fact 'Nazi' because the overt use of racism within the Punk Rock discourse marks the transformation of Oi! into so called 'white power rock and roll', a later stage in the dialectical unfolding of the discourse. Returning to the subject at hand, the Blaggers are not a typical Oi! band and only their early recordings can be placed within the genre. The group went on to integrate PUNK, rap and ska, using lots of samples to create a sound that enticed major label EMI to sign them up, although they were later dropped. The *Blag* (fun) side of their first album *On Yer Toez*, features standard Oi! lyrics such as 'Gonna go crazy if I don't go insane' and 'War on the terraces / Blood on the streets today.' The titles on the *Serious* side of the platter speak for themselves, *Jail House Doors, Freedom Fighters, Britain's Dream, Ireland, Greetings From Ireland, Save Your Hate* and *House Of The Fascist Scum.* The subject matter of these songs is too specific to fit in with the political rhetoric of Oi!, the Blaggers' ideological commitments are equally clear on *Victory To The ANC* or *It's Up To You*:

> Down in a city where a ghetto thrives / A concrete jungle where fear multiplies / Anger, frustration, are everywhere / Shotgun eyes blast a deadly glare / Time is now, they're coming for you / Time is now, it's up to you / It's up to you / Racist sadists in uniform / Think they can take the city by storm / The thin blue line wanna storm the streets / But the kids from the ghetto won't face defeat.

The Oppressed's first long player *Oi! Oi! Music*, a classic of this subgenre, is one of the best Skinhead records ever made. However, avoid their 1994 comeback album *We Can Do Anything*, which features nothing but PUNK and Oi! covers, because it's a real turkey. The band's sound is raw and crude but *Oi! Oi! Music* features one unlikely innovation, the use of electronic drums. Now don't fret, because the songs are dumbcore classics with archetypal Oi! lyrics, as is evident from the group's theme song *We're The Oppressed*:

> Born to fight / Born to win / We were all born to be Skins / Born with Martens on our feet / Face the truth there's no retreat / People fear us / Think we're strange / Boots and braces we won't change / We will never be second best / You know us we're the Oppressed / We are Skinheads / We are proud / Playing music for the crowd / Music for the working class / Stick your disco up your arse...

A handful of subjects recur in Oi! lyrics. These are violence, drinking, police oppression and references to Skinhead fashions. The lyrical concerns of a band like the Oppressed are so minimal that they make the Ramones look like Genesis. Another typical song is *Urban Soldiers*:

> Urban soldiers back out on the street / Kids in braces with their hair cropped neat / You don't know them but you know their name, Boot Boys, Suedeheads, they're all the same / Urban soldiers on the street / Urban soldiers kids you meet / Urban soldiers they don't run / Urban soldiers got no one / Coz they're Skinheads... up the town for a drink on Friday night / They'll be ready if you start a fight / They're the new breed and they get stuck in / Urban soldiers they're gonna win...

What lets the listener know this band is left-wing, or at least anti-racist, is the fact that they cover the old reggae standard *Skinhead Girl*, although they do PUNK it up. Oppressed singer Roddy Moreno is hated by Nazi Boneheads because he set up the British branch of Skinheads Against Racial Prejudice. However, beyond his stand against racism, there is little to differentiate Moreno's political outlook from that of the Bonehead bands since the ideology of both camps is largely rhetorical. Certainly, lyrics such as 'Magistrate, magistrate, you're the cunt we all hate' and 'The Tory party's got no soul / Three and a half million on the dole / Maggie's boys don't give a damn / About the plight of the working man,' are pretty standard Skinhead fare. The same is true of any of the Oppressed's songs, I'll give *Joe Hawkins* as a final example:

See him walking down the street / Doctor martens on his feet / Levi jeans, Ben Sherman shirt / Fuck with him and you'll get hurt / He's a Skinhead he don't care / Marten boots and short cropped hair / He's a Skinhead he don't care about you / Walking down on Brighton pier / Long haired hippies go in fear / Crunch of bone as the boot goes in / Joe's so proud to be a Skin... He isn't gonna change his ways / Skinhead's back it's here to stay / So if you think you've got the suss / Be a Skinhead be like us...

Now there can be little doubt that Roddy Moreno is basically a nice bloke who did everything he could to stamp out sectarianism and racism on the Skinhead scene. He sank some insurance money from a motor accident into the Oi! Records label, which issued product by everyone from the self-consciously left-wing Blaggers to Bonehead band Condemned 84. The latter group's mini-album *Battle Scarred*, put out by Moreno, boasted such Oi! classics as *Skinhead*, featuring the following words:

We wear our boots with pride and laces / Combat greens held up by braces / We've got our hair in a number one crop / We'll kick you in the head until you drop / We're on the streets looking for a fight / We're down the pub every night / We hate the Soulies, Mods and Teds / All we like is kicking heads / Skinhead, Skinheads, running in the night / Skinheads doing everyone in sight / We're all Skinheads through and through / We're all Skinheads who the fuck are you? / The Union Jack is our flag / And when we wear it / It makes us proud / And when the commies slag us down / We kick them all to the ground...

The other standout track on *Battle Scarred*, both musically and lyrically, was *Teenage Slag*:

If you pick on a nice young virgin / Will she be the best of the bunch? / Coz after you've laid her a few times / She'll like it ever so much / And then when you try some other position / She'll think it's so obscene / But she'll soon find out how good it is / And she'll still feel pure and clean / And she'll end up driving you mad / Probably end up with your dad / She's a teenage slag / After she's had a good time / She'll probably pass you by / And then all your mates and everybody / In the street will have a try / Passing round all the pubs / Get as many as she can / And when she's been round them all once / She'll go back round again...

Klaus Theweleit makes the following observation about Friekorps literature in *Male Fantasies Volume 1: Women, floods, bodies, history* (University of Minnesota Press, Minneapolis 1987) but it applies equally well to the song *Teenage Slag*:

> The description of the proletarian woman as a monster, as a beast, that unfortunately cannot be dealt with merely by 'planting a fist' in its 'ugly puss,' hardly derives from the actual behaviour of women in situations such as those described above (even here, they are hardly let off lightly). Rather, it can be traced to an attempt to construct a fantastic being who swears, shrieks, spits, scratches, farts, bites, pounces, tears to shreds; who is slovenly, wind-whipped, hissing-red, indecent; who whores around, slaps its naked thighs, and can't get enough of laughing at these men. In response to some secret need, this monster is identified with the proletarian woman...

Other Condemned 84 songs include *Gang Warfare, Keep The Faith, Face The Aggression, Strength To Strength, The Nutter, Oi! Ain't Dead, We Will Never Die, The Boots Go Marching In, Kick Down The Doors, Our Time Will Come, Warriors With Pride, In The Gutter, All Out Attack* and *Pride And The Pain*. It seems, at times, as if the band are obsessively driven to assert their masculinity because this is the only way in which they are able to reinforce the extremely vague boundaries that mark off their bodies, gender, identity, sexuality. Since Condemned 84 were Boneheads rather than Skinheads, it was no great surprise when they completely abandoned the Oi! subgenre and adopted a heavy metal musical style on their 1992 album *Storming To Power*. Heavy metal, in terms of appearance at least, is more self-consciously 'white' and 'male' than the PUNK ROCK genre, which carries within it a provocative ambiguity, as we shall see as we examine its four stage unfolding.

A band whose musical 'development/degeneration' followed a remarkably similar pattern to that of Condemned 84 is Close Shave. While neither band used racist lyrics on vinyl, both favoured a rhetorical nationalism and Close Shave were even willing to play on the same bill as openly Nazi bands; in the past they have gigged with Skrewdriver. Nevertheless, the comic book approach on songs such as *Sunday Sport* make early Close Shave recordings typical Oi! fodder:

> Sex and scandal all the way / It's the paper for you on a Sunday / All the slags and the old bags / Showing their tits in the Sunday rag / Maria Whitaker bearing her all / Great big tits of Tina Small / Well

these girls they can't be real / I for one wouldn't mind a feel, Oi! / Sunday Sport, it's the Sunday Sport / Don't get caught with the Sunday Sport / Girls with big tits on the cover / Don't you show it to your mother / Buy the paper every Sunday morn / In the paper rack amongst the porn / Centre spread goes straight to my head / I wanna get them into my bed / There's the letters from the readers wives / Telling the stories of their kinky lives / The agony aunt is Fiona Wright / She knows what to do in the night, alright!

If the group's first long player *Oi! Kinnock Give Us Back Our Rose!* sounded musically incompetent and was very poorly produced, it nevertheless worked within the context of the PUNK ROCK genre, whose devotees are predisposed to considering raw and absurdly premature recordings to be not only highly desirable, but a mark of ideological distinction. By the time they recorded their second album, *Hard As Nails*, Close Shave sounded like a competent rock band, although the lyrics remained absurdly infantile:

It would solve a lot of problems / If death was enforced here / It would put the shit up murders, rapists and the queers / If death was made the sentence / Then sex crimes they may drop / The pervert would be no more / And that would be no loss / Death row, death row / Just four walls nowhere to go / Waiting for the day that you meet your maker / You're in a cell on death row / An alternative to prison at the rate-payers loss / A noose around the neck or an electric shock / What gives a man a right to live / If he takes another's life? / He's killed once, he'll kill again / So lets end this bastard's life... Standing in a court room the verdict it is death / He killed an innocent person / Put a cord around his neck / It happens all the time on American city streets / Murders, rapes and muggings / Keep Britain free from this...

Oi! is sometimes called street rock by those immersed in the discourse, but despite the rhetoric about knowing the 'reality' of living on council estates surrounded by the constant threat of violence and crime, in songs such as *Red Light Girl*, Close Shave leave the casual listener with the impression that they subsist in a cotton wool world:

Staring at the punters in their cars / Blowing them a kiss and flashing your arse / Giving them an address so you can meet / In a dark house on a lonely street / Straining in your wig in a looking glass / Ready for a dildo up your arse / Bloke comes in and he looks so tough / Says he wants you to play it rough / Red light girl you're living a lie / Wrecking the lives of your husbands and wives / Red light girl I want you to know / Using your body while you're breaking the law / Social security you could get by / You could get a job if you really tried / No need to use your body for a job / Go out cheating for the working slobs / Black shiny leather bondage stripes and whips / Pick the wrong bloke and you've had your chips / Going to the men do you like what you see? / Do you get nicked by the CID?

The term do-gooder is usually applied to liberals but in an equally derogatory fashion it makes perfect sense to affix it to Close Shave. The band's absurd rhetorical defence of family values is so completely entangled with their repressed fantasies and fears they often end up celebrating the very things that they imagine they are against. There is a great deal of unconscious humour here and one is not laughing with the band, but at them. By the time of their third long player, *Lone Riders*, Close Shave had abandoned the Oi! subgenre for heavy metal and were singing about *Alfred The Great* and *Insomnia*. No doubt the singer spent a great many sleepless nights pondering the strange desires he felt towards other men. The group had already thanked 'a self-confessed gay' for his help and support on a previous album.

One band that didn't degenerate into a heavy metal outfit was Combat 84. This was partly because only the singer, 'Nazi Chris Henderson', was an extremely sad bastard, but also thanks to the fact that they broke up during the recording of their first album. The band appeared on a TV documentary with upper class windbag 'Nazi Chris' doing a ham impersonation of a racist 'yob', while the guitarist was very articulate in expressing his anti-racist beliefs. After the programme was broadcast, venues cancelled gigs and Combat 84 were forced to call it a day. The group's music was brickwall Oi! and their theme song, a classic example of the subgenre, runs as follows:

Ten hole DMs on your feet / Well polished and looking neat / Paramilitary is the score / We're the band Combat 84 / Come on you Skinheads / No-one's safe when we walk by / That's why we won't fade and die / Short hair and braces hanging down / There'll always be a Skinhead in town / That's why we rule the street / That's why we've gotta be discreet... Skinheads will never die!

It should go without saying that Combat 84 wrote and performed a song called *Skinhead*:

We will never fade and die / Whatever you try to do / We're the first of today / And the last of tomorrow / Skinhead's not a fashion / It's a way of life / Skinhead, Skinhead never give up / Stick together and act as one / You never never never give up / You stick together and act as one / You see us on the telly / You read about us in the news / We will never fade and die / Whatever you try to do...

While there was nothing deliberately offensive about this or several other songs, 'Nazi Chris' hoped to wind people up with ditties such as *Right To Choose*:

Fuck off CND / The end of the world is coming in too / We are ready to fight - are you? / When you're on your knees with a gun to your head / It's better to be dead than fucking red / We have the right, the right to choose / We want defence and we want the Cruise / They gave their lives and they bled / Remember the Falklands don't forget our dead / The right to choose, we want the Cruise / The right to choose, we want the Cruise / Bigger and better bombs!

However, rather than winding up lefties, 'Nazi Chris' pissed off his mates on the far-Right. Rumour provides us with one of the best thick Bonehead stories of all time and it doesn't really matter whether or not it's literally true because despite his exclusive Charterhouse education, the Combat 84 singer doesn't have two brain cells to rub together. The band put *Right To Choose* out on their own Victory label and 'Nazi Chris' took it along to the National Front's White Noise Club to see if this outfit would distribute it. The record was given the thumbs down because the NF opposed what they described as 'American imperialism', believing that 'foreign' Cruise missiles should be removed from Britain's shores and replaced with our own 'independent' nuclear deterrent! In fact, British and American military operations are so entangled that this position was as absurd as the rest of the National Front's pathetic programme.

Henderson had really screwed up because the fascist White Noise Club doubtlessly loved *Rapist*, the A-side of this maxi-single:

He's a dirty and evil man / Who no one wants to know / He could be living in your town / Coz the sign of the rapist doesn't show / Young girls come to me / Stalking victims in the street / When it happens no one sees / You're just dragged down off your feet / Capital punishment / Stronger government / Plastic mask and hairy wig / You're too scared to show your face / You're acting like a dirty pig / You're a cancer of the human race / Filth of society should all die / We need a stronger government / All you've gotta do is hang 'em high / Bring back capital punishment / Capital punishment / A stronger government / We need a stronger government / Bring back capital punishment... Hang 'em, hang 'em, hang 'em high / You watch those fucking bastards die... Capital punishment / Stronger government!

Although Henderson gave up music to concentrate on being an amateur football hooligan and full time idiot, it comes as no surprise to learn that the group's second drummer went on to join heavy metal outfit April 19th. Another Oi! idol who attempted to pursue a career on the HM scene was Millwall Roi Pearce, formerly of the Last Resort and the 4 Skins. The Last Resort had specialised in cod nationalism and their song *Red, White And Blue* was a masterpiece of rhetorical underkill:

> England, England is my land / It's the only place I understand / From Carlisle down to the Dover Straits / Our forefathers made us great / All that's true is the red, the white and blue / You took us in Europe it wasn't our choice / We the people must have our voice / No other flag will hold us back / Because our flag's the Union Jack / All that's true is the red, the white and blue / Call us hooligans, call us yobs / In the war its us that do the job / No other country will make us slaves / Britannia will rule the waves / All that's true is the red, the white and blue.

Now it doesn't take a 'genius' to work out that by using Carlisle and Dover as marker points in the lyric, Pearce is demarcating England. Logically the blue of Scotland should be excluded from the lyric but then 'all that's true is the red and the white' wouldn't scan and lacks emotive impact. When the Last Resort broke up after recording their first album, Pearce became the last singer to handle vocals for the 4 Skins. At the end of the eighties he put together a new band called the Resort and on a tune entitled *Rock 'N' Roll* declared: 'Back street heroes are dead and gone / We have no intention of the same old song / We was caught up in political rows / Now we're in control it's rock 'n' roll now.' The Resorts' *1989* album is an attempt at making mainstream rock and doesn't belong within the Oi! subgenre, the group didn't last long in any case.

In 1992, Pearce made another stab at a musical career with the Heavy Metal Outlaws who released two maxi-singles before folding. The first of these bore the title *Sex For Sexism's Sake* and featured the classic *Get Your Tits Out*:

> Ever since I was eight years old / I was a fan of the centrefold / Girl's good looking, she's got class / Stick my cock right up her arse / Me mate's doing time or so I heard / So I'm going round there to shag

his bird / Don't like oral makes her sick / Never mind slag get on my dick / Come on the heat I'm a sex machine / I'm a really going down like a submarine / Girl next door she just don't care / Gonna get buried in her pubic hair / She's got long legs and wears pink socks / I've had my tongue right up her box / I know nice wenches, some pretty maids / You gotta be careful you don't catch AIDS / Get them home and back to their place / Get them upstairs and come in their face... Bend me, break me, any way you take me / All you've gotta do is masturbate me!

This was an attempt to cross rap, heavy metal and PUNK, with 'sexism' being the ideological point at which they were all supposed to meet. Of course, as a consumer come on, it failed miserably, although it did at least prove that not every 'patriotic' Bonehead is destined to turn into a racist bore. It is nevertheless unfortunate that most Oi! 'musicians' who failed to introduce elements of ska into their sound ended up embracing some form of Grease, that old enemy of the original hard Mods who mutated into Skinheads back in the sixties.

Anyone who (mis)reads this text as containing an account of Skinheadism will already have a very lopsided view of that particular subculture. In these pages I am dealing with PUNK ROCK as a musical genre, of which Oi! is just one strand. It should be equally obvious from what I've written that Oi! is simply one element in a broad spectrum of Skinhead musical tastes, which also embrace ska and soul. Since Oi! is particularly attractive to Boneheads, who are neither Boot Boys nor Grease but a cross between the two, this particular musical subgenre is very unrepresentative of Skinhead culture in general and inferences about the latter cannot be drawn from the former. It should not need restating that Oi! became the standard form of 'ideological' Punk Rock during one phase of its dialectical unfolding. And having qualitatively transformed Punk Rock by quantitatively increasing the level of 'proletarian' rhetoric in and around the genre, Oi! was overwhelmed by something else altogether, as its emphasis on a 'working class' identity became increasingly 'racial' in nature...

VIII

HAIL HAIL ROCK 'N' ROLL
Skrewdriver and the degeneration of the Punk
Rock dialectic

If the dialectic I am describing appears crude, that is simply a reflection of my subject matter which is neither intellectually sophisticated nor receptive to self-consciously complex cultural forms. However, while Oi! provided its audience with a parodic vision of what it was to be 'British and working class' in the early eighties, this does not necessarily imply that it was simply a joke; the categories 'serious' and 'not serious' aren't really applicable to the subgenre. Oi! orientates itself in a very different manner to the ideological dogma of high culture and it is absurd to project philosophical notions derived from the latter modes of belief onto an unrelated set of phenomena.

Some readers may feel that I come across as suspiciously anti-Bergsonian, holding to the position that time is not real, that all events are merely the unfolding of a reality already existent in the world. If this is so, it is merely an unfortunate by-product of my current engagement with the Punk Rock discourse, which in retrospect appears to have been completely (pre)determined. Since wo/man exists in language, only those who master semiotic codes rise above determinism to heroically assert their free will. If, like Bergson, we dispense with the notion that real time is homogeneous then there is no difficulty in explaining why a band like Close Shave could produce classic slabs of Oi! in the late eighties. Of course, I could just as easily state that 'late' manifestations of Oi! were produced by individuals who had been left behind by the World-Spirit, but it would be difficult to reconcile such a position with genre theory. The point I'm making is that it's too easy to reduce things to neat but absurdly reductive categories. Instead of attempting to reduce PUNK ROCK to a series of static positions, we must grasp its movement.

As Oi! developed, the subgenre's insistence on propagating a nostalgic vision of what it was to be working class, alongside its desire to posit this in terms of a mythologised British identity, led to an increasing interest in the issue of race. However, once the idea of 'racial nationalism' is sung about openly, quantity is transformed into quality and instead of Oi! we are confronted with 'white power rock and roll'. This is the next stage of our dialectic, within ideological Punk Rock the focus of concern has shifted from rhetoric about class into the most bestial manifestation of race hate. In mystical terms, Earth has been transformed into Water. It is a cliché to state that water always finds its own level, and it should go without saying that in the case of 'white power rock and roll' this is deep beneath the Earth. Instead of being a source of life, this water has absorbed lethal amounts of poison and now festers in a dank cavern deep underground.

Although there have been many Nazi Bonehead bands, given the Fuhrer principle it is only necessary to deal in any depth with the leading exponents of 'white power rock and roll.' Skrewdriver were not so much a band as a person, middle class grammar schoolboy Ian Stuart, whose evolution into a seriously sad bastard peddling a particularly idiotic brand of race hate is a story of cowardice and indecision. In 1977 Skrewdriver emerged out of a Rolling Stones cover band called Tumbling Dice who had been active in the Blackpool suburb of Poulton-Le-Fylde since the end of 1975. Much to their later embarrassment, the independent label Chiswick provided Skrewdriver with both a record contract and a name. Roger Armstrong explains how he came to sign the band in the booklet accompanying the double CD set *The Chiswick Story* (Ace, London 1992):

> Skrewdriver didn't even have a name when they sent in a demo tape to Chiswick, so one was invented. They were bitter, crude, impassioned and not that fashion conscious. Four lads from Blackpool up in 'the Smoke' and no big advance, but at least they had a record out. *You're So Dumb...* The B-side of the next Skrewdriver single was a tribute to singer Ian's favourite group the Rolling Stones. Here we are in 1977 – 'no Elvis, Beatles or the Rolling Stones' and Skrewdriver are murdering *19th Nervous Breakdown*. The A-side *Anti-Social...* was one of the most simplistic, brutal punk records ever made. The first album *All Skrewed Up...* came out and was played so fast it had to be cut at 45 rpm. With twelve tracks and a short running time it was sold at mid-price... Singer Ian eventually joined an obscure British cult. NB: Because of Ian's later activities and the fact that he continued to use the band's name we have regretfully omitted any Skrewdriver material from the compilation, though the songs in themselves were fairly typical punk rants of the days and gave no insights into the unfortunate associations that the band's name

developed later. None of the other members of the band became involved in any such activities.

The most amusing thing about the picture sleeves of the first two Skrewdriver singles is that the band are shown to be punk hicks with longish hair. The barnets had been cropped by the time of the photo session for their album *All Skrewed Up*, which has the opening lines of the old reggae song *Skinhead Moonstomp* scrawled across the back cover. Now, if Roger Armstrong is embarrassed about what his young protégé went on to do, then Ian Stuart's later apologists have to make excuses for Skrewdriver's early output. National Front jailbird Joe Pearce put it this way in his booklet *Skrewdriver: The First Ten Years, The Way It's Got To Be!*:

> The shallow nihilism of *Anti-Social*, *I Don't Like You* and *I Don't Need Your Love* on side one of *All Skrewed Up* are counter-balanced by *9 Till 5* and the excellent *(Too Much) Confusion* on side two. These last two tracks, together with *Government Action* on side one, indicate through their lyrical content the birth of Ian Stuart's political awareness.

Yes indeed, one can see the political maturity in the words of *(Too Much) Confusion*:

> All the councillors in Blackpool / With their poxy bars / Why don't you fuck off / You're much too old to persecute us / And just think about that local publicity huh? / Thank you / Too much confusion / Too much confusion / Too much confusion around here / Well can you hear those Labour rats spouting shit? / Well you ain't too convincing / You can't fool everybody / All the violence / All the reporters snivelling around / Tomorrow's headlines / We all know whose gonna get the blame, don't we?... There's so many people condemning me / They're just trying to dictate / Tell me what to think / Well I don't need your press / I don't need your write ups / And I don't need your put downs / So just go and mess up someone else's life will ya?

Jailbird Joe Pearce shares an uncanny ability with Groovy Greil Marcus: both are able to find profundity and intellectual sophistication when there's none around. Personally, I can't see much difference between the lyrical content of *(Too Much) Confusion* and what Pearce condemns as the 'nihilism' of *Anti-Social*:

> Adding up figures and reading books / Getting sick blinkin' sucks / I don't wanna listen to another word / I'm so bleedin' bored / I'm anti-social, anti-social, anti-social / I hate the world / I don't wanna go work another day / Wanna be somebody / I don't wanna wear no three piece suits / I don't want a family / Coz I'm anti-social...

Wandering round the streets you tell me what to do / Thinking of
the dole queue line / I ain't got no money or a settled will / It's a
bloody drag / Looking at the posers in their flashy cars / I'm just
walking round / Never gonna get a wife / Have some kids / I ain't
gonna settle down / Coz I'm anti-social...

Since Groovy Greil Marcus is one drift short of a situation, it's
only Skrewdriver's leper status that prevents him from claiming
them as Situationists, 'wandering round the streets' must sound
remarkably like psychogeography to a 'contemporary cultural critic'.
Meanwhile, jailbird Joe Pearce is left with no choice but to completely ignore early Skrewdriver songs such as *Jailbait*:

> Normal hair looks so good / Temptation think I should? / Jailbait,
> jailbait, jailbait / No one knows you're sneaking out / Your old man
> would scream and shout / Jailbait, jailbait, jailbait / Just because
> you're just fifteen / They can't guess the things you've seen / Jailbait,
> jailbait, jailbait / They don't want you getting pissed / Enjoying things
> that they have missed / Jailbait, jailbait, jailbait.

Another song recorded in 1977 that Pearce doesn't mention,
probably because he's a convert to Roman Catholicism, is *Unbe-
liever*: 'I believe in violence / That's the only way / Make people
see our problems / Don't let them fade away / So I said I don't
believe in Jesus / When will I see him now?' Prescient, or what?

Roger Armstrong is right, this is typical 1977 PUNK ROCK fodder;
beyond the rhetoric about youth, the main lyrical thrust is towards
individualism, often expressed through negative posturing about
'anti-social' behaviour. It cannot be emphasised enough that this is
pure theatrics, there's nothing here that deserves much consider-
ation, it's just good old fashioned dirty teenage fun. Ian Stuart
summed up his beliefs at that time with the song *The Only One*:
'Never reckoned much to mixing / People always messed me
round / Always looking out for favours / Try to bleed me into the
ground / Coz God I'm the loner baby / God I'm the only one...' In
fact, given that this song appears to have a centred-subject, whereas
(Too Much) Confusion is a sea of shifting perspectives, with different
audiences being addressed during the course of the number, it
seems most sensible to posit an unreflective and narcissistic nihilism as being the world view that dominated Stuart's 'thinking' during the late seventies. Ultimately, Skrewdriver's 1977 Chiswick releases were dumbcore at its dumbest.

97

Having released *All Skrewed Up* in November 1977, Chiswick lost interest in the band whose indifferent sales indicated they were going nowhere fast. The single *Streetfighter*, scheduled for April 1978 release, was never issued. Skrewdriver carried on gigging for a few months but never graduated out of tiny club venues such as the Roxy and Vortex, eventually splitting up in the summer of 1978 when Ian Stuart returned to Blackpool to work in a car wash. Stuart dropped out of sight, not to be heard from again until a letter appeared in the *Melody Maker* of 29 September 1979:

> I am writing to inform you that the biased information that has appeared recently in your paper, and which RAR seem to be responsible for, is false. The news that Skrewdriver were reforming to do NF gigs is complete and utter bullshit. I formed the band and finally split it up over a year ago. I rarely see the other members of the group and have no intention of forming a band with any of them again. Where RAR get their information beats me. Maybe they have a little KGB-type organisation in their ranks. To suggest that we have come out in favour of the NF is also a lie. I've never voted NF and have no interest whatsoever in politics, and never had. I've also been told that RAR has solid links with the Anti-Nazi League, an organisation who, it seems, are backed heavily by the communist and Marxist parties, who in their way are just as much of a threat to this country as the NF or BM. Why don't the two sides go and battle out their political wars in Hyde Park or somewhere, and let the people who just want to have a good time and hear some music do so in peace, without being pestered by people pushing either communism or fascism? I'm at present forming a new band which is not called Skrewdriver, and don't intend doing gigs for the RAR, NF or any other political organisation.

In fact, at the time he wrote the letter Ian Stuart was Young National Front organiser for Blackpool and Fylde, having joined the organisation after returning north from London in the summer of 1978. Stuart had met up with Young National Front boss and notorious jailbird Joe Pearce at the Hoop And Grapes pub, in London's Farringdon Street, to discuss the possibility of reforming Skrewdriver to play NF gigs, and this was the source of the rumours that the car wash attendant was hell bent on denying. Still hoping for a career in the music business, Stuart had decided that singing for the Front might ruin his chances of chart success. He was to dream about that big record deal for the rest of his life, in a 1993 interview with the fanzine *Last Chance* he is quoted as saying: 'Obviously I would like to have made a lot of money and been on *Top Of The Pops* and all that, what other person who's been in a band wouldn't... If I went to the press and told them I've changed my ways I could be on *Top Of The Pops*.' Yes, it's that old 'I could have been a contender' speech.

Instead of singing for his supper at National Front rallies as the seventies receded into the realm of memory, Stuart and Skrewdriver bassist Kevin McKay moved to Manchester to reform the band with new boys Glen Jones and Martin Smith. However, after a year of northern gigs and the release of a maxi single on the independent TJM label, Stuart realised that Skrewdriver's reputation was even lower in Manchester than it had been in London two years previously, and the band broke up again. Bearing this in mind, the A-side of the one single the group managed to release at this time, *Built Up Knocked Down*, appears particularly ironic:

> The summer was coming on, I was out in the fields / Then I heard a guitar playing, loud and clear / I saw an old man sat by a tree / He said come and listen to me son, come and listen to me / He said what does life mean to you / Does it mean go out get drunk, drown your blues? / He said, if that's what it means to you / Well that's a waste of life and I've got nothing more to say to you / Quit my job and I went out, I bought my first guitar / Then I started to learn that thing / Instead of propping up a bar / Sent a tape, got our contract, made us all so glad / Then they started messing round, now life's as bad / Are you trying to mess us up, trying to make us quit / If that's what you're trying to do, you're not achieving it / Built up, knocked down, knocked down to the ground.

Ian Stuart returned to Blackpool where he worked for his dad until he moved down to London to take up employment as a cycle courier and reside in a hostel that was used by the DHSS as a temporary dumping ground for the homeless. Stuart never had much initiative and always needed someone else to manage the business side of things for him, and so it took the encouragement of Mickey French, proprietor of Skinhead clobber shop the Last Resort, to get him to reform Skrewdriver yet again. This time, Stuart was the only survivor from the previous line-up. French issued Skrewdriver's next single *Back With A Bang* on his own Last Resort Sounds label in 1982 with a re-recording of the album track *I Don't Like You* on the B-side, because the band was seriously short of new material and no record company would touch them. Stuart still wasn't ready to go openly Nazi, he simply wanted to test the water by hinting at his political beliefs:

> Do you remember in the summer / Back in 1978 / When they reckoned that the Skinheads days were numbered / And the papers dripped with liquid hate / Being patriotic's not the fashion so they say / To fly your country's flag's a crime / Society tried it's best to kill you / But the spirit lives until the end of time / Coz we're back with a bang now / Back with the gang now / Back with a bang now / Run with the gang now...

Once again, Stuart was aiming for an audience who were so lumpen that their theatrical notion of what it was to be 'working class' led them to pretend that they'd never heard of *Last Night At The Proms* where they could have waved as many Union Jacks as their little hearts desired, and no one would have bothered them. However, in fairness, I should state that this would have presented them with a major 'intellectual' challenge since they'd then have had to find something else to whinge about. Although *Back With A Bang* is a competent slice of headbanging PUNK ROCK, it didn't surprise anyone that the song failed to make the national charts. Once again, Ian Stuart found himself peddling the Skrewdriver live act in tiny venues such as that cramped basement on Oxford Street known as the 100 Club. He was back where he'd left off four years earlier when he'd first quit the music business, although this time he at least had the safety net of a day job as a cycle courier.

French issued a couple more Skrewdriver tracks on the *United Skins* compilation album he threw together, a re-recording of *Anti-Social* and a newer song called *Boot And Braces* which included such 'classic' lines as: 'Try and get you banned from everywhere / Coz you wear your boots and you cut your hair / They would rather see you in a dirty old kaftan / If you were a hippie baby you won't face no ban.' *Anti-Social* lacked the brickwall production of the Chiswick single and the only thing to make up for this was the addition of a new verse: 'I ain't gonna be no rich man's fool / I ain't gonna perm my hair / Gonna wear boots and the shortest crop / Watch the straights all stare.' Here we can see the influence of Oi!, something that Stuart had to take up, internalise and transform before he could shift ideological Punk Rock from it's class based phase into the unfolding of its latent racial content. This entailed a number of reversals, it would take innumerable record releases before these could be fully worked out and replaced by something that was much

100

too healthy for Stuart to openly express, only Queercore and Riot Grrrl could do that. Joe Pearce quotes Stuart as saying:

> The press slagged us off for coming out with 'ultra-nationalist' comments from the stage. They called our audience 'morons'. In the end I just got fed up. It was obvious they were never going to praise us for anything, and in any case I couldn't see anything wrong with being a nationalist, it was natural to me. That's when we thought we might as well go the whole way.

Stuart had never intended to take a political stand, he'd just wanted a career in the music industry, it took him five years to realise he was a talentless hack who might as well exploit the shock value of musical fascism. Like most bigots, Stuart's political views were always completely incoherent, as we shall see.

The next Skrewdriver release was the *White Power* maxi-single on the National Front's newly founded White Noise label:

> I stand and watch my country going down the drain / We are all at fault now, we are all to blame / We're letting them take over, we just let them come / Once we had an Empire, and now we've got a slum / White power for Britain / White power today / White power for England / Before it gets too late / We've seen a lot of riots, we just sit and scoff / We've seen a lot of muggings, and the judges let them off... We've got to do something to try and stop the rot / The traitors that abused us, they should all be shot / Are we going to sit and let them come? / Have they got the white man on the run? / Multiracial society is a mess / Ain't gonna take much more of this / What do we need? / White power... If we don't win our battle, and all does not go well / It's apocalypse for Britain, and we'll see you all in Hell

White Power was neither inspired nor inspiring, it had a weedy sound due to its inept production and the only level on which it could possibly work was as a novelty record, because the entire thing was so obviously a joke. Clearly, the slogan 'white power', a completely vacuous and abstract demand that can have no meaning whatsoever in a country that already has a 'white' ruling class, was derived, via George Lincoln Rockwell, from notions of black power. Without the idea of black power, it would not be possible to arrive at the 'concept' of 'white power' and this is precisely why 'white power' was not used as a slogan by pre-war fascist groups. Not only were Skrewdriver playing multi-cultural rock music, but after becoming openly racist, they quickly dropped the 'up-tight' style of punk, which actually reflects socially constructed notions of what it is to be 'white', and instead adopted a more blues based form of rock instrumentation. Likewise, in his lyrics, Stuart became increasingly concerned with portraying 'whites' as an oppressed minority who exude warmth. In other words, Stuart adopted a world view in which 'whites' came to take on all the characteristics that are customarily associated with culturally constructed notions of 'blackness'. Of course, it's very easy to demonise an individual with Stuart's absurd views, but it only takes a little bit of reflection to realise that such a reaction tends to reinforce the delusions suffered by someone tormented by this type of mental illness. A paranoid viewpoint was plainly exhibited on the next Skrewdriver single *Voice Of Britain*:

> Walking round the streets, hand in hand with fear / Nobody knows what is round the bend / Don't side with the other side coz if you do we'll find you / We want to know if you classify as friends / This is the voice, the voice of Britain / And you'd better believe it / This is the voice, the voice of Britain / C'mon and fly the flag / It's a time when our old people cannot walk the street alone / Fought for this country is this all they get back / Risked their lives for Britain, now Britain belongs to aliens / It's about time the British went and took their Britain back... Now we'll have a go at the TV and the papers / And all the media Zionists who like to keep us quiet / They're trying to bleed our country, they're the leeches of the nation / But we won't give up quietly, we're going to stand and fight...

Paranoia is equally evident on other tracks from the same period, such as *On The Streets*: 'Walking down the subway at the weekend / After a good night out on the town / There's gangs over here, gangs over there, there's gangs everywhere / You'd better watch out if you're on your own'. These lyrics do not portray the views of a tough, centred, self-confident individual, but instead display the bunker mentality of a cowed and cringing coward failing dismally in 'his' desperate attempts to prove that 'he' is a 'man'. However, the really important lyrical 'developments' in terms of the unfolding of the Punk Rock dialectic weren't to be found in a mature form until Skrewdriver recorded their album *Hail The New Dawn*. The notion of race embraced by Stuart leads on into highly formalised rituals of male bonding, which are verbally articulated in terms of 'pride' and 'loyalty'. We are beginning to see the emergence of a love that dare not speak its name, most obviously on the track *Our Pride Is Our Loyalty* whose lyrics unconsciously betray the fact that the goose-step is really a 'pansy twist'. As Ian Stuart becomes increasingly desperate to assert his masculinity, it continually eludes him, slips away and is replaced by the very opposite of heterosexuality; quantity is transformed into quality and regardless of the singer's refusal to openly admit the fact, it becomes patently obvious that the bloke is a 'cream puff'.

By the time *Hail The New Dawn* was released, Ian Stuart had already developed his 'close relationship' with Nicky Crane, who wrote the lyrics for the track *Justice* and organised 'security' at Skrewdriver concerts. Crane, of course, later renounced fascism and came out as openly gay a year or so before his death from AIDS. Crane's public proclamation of his sexuality was widely reported in the press, as well as being the subject of a TV documentary. Under the headline *Reformed Fascist Ready To Admit Homosexuality*, the *Independent* of 27 July 1992 reported:

> Nicky Crane is a changed man... But if his defection from the fervently anti-gay ranks of the Skinhead movement will be a blow to its pride, it is only the most celebrated sign of a thriving gay subculture in the traditionally homophobic Skinhead scene. Not only are long-time Skinheads 'coming out' but the image is being adopted by a growing number of men in the gay community.

Of course, Crane was close to many 'white power rock and roll' bands. The group 'No Remorse' are another interesting case in point, their album *The New Storm Troopers* is dedicated to Nicky Crane and at least one other openly gay man, despite the fact that the chorus to the song *We Play For You* runs as follows: 'We don't play for no red students / We don't play for no Jews / We don't play for no homosexuals / We play for you.' In terms of the ideology they profess, the membership of 'No Remorse' harbour all sorts of shameful secrets. These, of course, include the long list of their 'shirt-lifting' friends. Some 'No Remorse' fans might be surprised by the intensity of the male bonding that goes on between the group and its German 'brothers'. The singer Paul Bellany aka Paul Burnley, and his brother Jonathan, who has played drums for Skrewdriver, are the sons of Scottish painter John Bellany who was awarded a CBE in 1994. The privileged upbringing these two bozos enjoyed cuts against the rhetoric about the 'white working class' pumped out by the bands they've 'played with', and they are equally appalled by papa's 'degenerate' art and political opinions. Daddy has been quoted by the national press as saying 'I detest racism, I loathe it'.

Returning to Skrewdriver, after *Hail The New Dawn*, which saw them moving away from a PUNK ROCK sound, they completely abandoned the genre in favour of 'rock' music, although they remained deeply unsure of where they were going, a state of affairs that reflected Ian Stuart's schizophrenic mental state. On the *Blood & Honour* album they wanted to play competent mainstream rock, but merely come across as mediocre. In terms of idiocy, the standout track was *Prisoner Of Peace*:

> Free Rudolf Hess / How long can they keep him there we can only guess... And now the situation has changed in many ways / The allies want to let him go they've decided he has paid / The red scum in the Kremlin with their kosher malice try / To keep a proud man locked away until the day he dies / Free Rudolf Hess / How long can they keep him there we can only guess / He's a prisoner of peace / Kept there at the will of the Marxists in the east...

Less than two years after *Blood & Honour* was released in December 1985, the Nazi war criminal died in his prison cell, thereby reinforcing Ian Stuart's easily won status as a paranoid political loser. To give an indication of the sterility of the milieu in which Skrewdriver moved, it's worth quoting a small portion of Joe Pearce's blow by blow account of the tracks on the *Blood & Honour* long player:

> *One Fine Day*... is somewhat profound making it more like the product of some art student rather than the leader of a down-to-earth Skinhead rock band. 'Yeah, man, far out,' Ian laughs when I put this to him. Seriously though, *One Fine Day* does make a valid, albeit a subtle point. Ian explains 'I wrote that quite some time ago actually. I was reading through the paper and it was a really beautiful day, sun shining, hot, and a clear blue sky, and there was nothing in the paper but death and destruction all over the world. It just struck me as being something to write about.' *Searching*, the fourth track on side two, is arguably the heaviest on the album and certainly it is the most proximate to the classic heavy metal sound which *Blood & Honour* epitomises and which Skrewdriver as a group were evolving towards. This being so it is perhaps no surprise that it is one of Ian Stuart's favourite tracks on the album. 'That's another 'profound' statement!' Ian explains jokingly about the lyrics of *Searching*, still amused at my observation of the preceeding track. 'It's basically about what you're looking for in life and will you ever find it. Most people never do. They always consider that they have certain goals in life but when they reach them they want something else. Nobody really knows what

they are actually looking for I don't think.' Profound indeed! G. K. Chesterton in Doctor Marten's boots!

The next album was the equally mediocre *White Rider* and that was followed by the even more abysmal *After The Fire*, which included covers of Lynyrd Skynyrd's *Sweet Home Alabama* and a truly awful rendition of the folk song *Green Fields Of France*. Musically, Stuart didn't have a clue where he was going. By this time, Skrewdriver had fallen out with Patrick Harrington and Derek Holland, their chums who ran the National Front White Noise Club, and the 'odd couple' provided the subject matter for their song *A Time Of Change*:

> Stood against us are the scum / They are worried because their time will come / One calls himself a revolutionary, turned out to be a gay / Just a mummy's little rich boy / It's a time of change / It's a time of change / They call themselves political soldiers but they have a massive yellow streak / A soldier has strength but they are bent, limp wristed and weak / Pathetic little mummy's boys there was nothing they wanted for / But come the day when they have to pay, we'll see who they were working for / The other enemy he held aloft a cross / And in his church that day he prayed to be the boss / But all he wanted was money / And all he wanted was praise / Now he's gone and the bands play on / It's a time of change...

In the pages of the *Blood & Honour* newsletter and elsewhere in print, Stuart accused Harrington and Holland of using the White Noise Club to rip-off Skrewdriver's money. The paranoid singer already considered himself to have been metaphorically 'fucked up the arse' by Chiswick Records and Mickey French of the Last Resort shop, and one is left wondering if his infinitely deeper hatred for Harrington stems from some more physical attachment. Which brings us back to the transformation of quantity in quality in the four stage unfolding of ideological Punk Rock, because with their lyrical emphasis on pride, loyalty, comradeship and 'brothers across the sea', the exaggerated masculinity of the 'white power rock and roll' bands was transformed into its opposite. Thus within the Punk Rock discourse, the rhetorical organising principle shifts from class, to race, to sexuality and gender; or, if you prefer, after Earth and poisoned Water, we can breath the pure Air of Queercore and Riot Grrrl.

However, before moving on, let's just get the history of Skrewdriver out of the way. On the *Warlord* long player, Stuart was still looking for a musical direction, and the weedy version of AC/DC's *Back In Black* provided the answer. On *The Strong Survive*, Skrewdriver finally went completely HM, with lame covers of *United* by Judas Priest and the very aptly chosen *Paranoid* by Black Sabbath. This was followed by the unlistenable *Live And Kicking* double album, which was recorded through a mixing desk at a concert and then, judging by the sound quality, the tape was flushed down a toilet before being retrieved. Here, Ian Stuart's complete lack of ideological consistence is highlighted by a cover of Chuck Berry's *Johnny B. Goode*, with the lyrics changed to *Johnny Joined The Klan*. Skrewdriver not only played multi-cultural music, they even covered a song written by a black rocker as part of their attempt to spread white racism. They also murdered *Sweet Home Alabama* yet again, all in all yet another lame, and unconscious, 'outing'. In 1992 Skrewdriver released *Freedom What Freedom*, featuring such utterly uninspired tracks as *What Price Freedom*:

> Don't care too much for Tories / Labour wants to flood this land / Don't care too much for Liberals / With their wishy-washy plans / I just care for my country and the people who belong / Because I'm proud to say it the public ban this song / And I said what price freedom in this world today / What price freedom what am I allowed to say...

Ian Stuart was sounding both very tired and very paranoid. He was put out of his misery by his death in a car crash on 24 September 1993. Fortunately, to date, only one posthumous Skrewdriver album has been released. I don't need to deal with Stuart's solo work or his output with the Klansman and White Diamond because these fall outside the PUNK ROCK genre.

By pushing the notion of 'white' 'masculinity' to an extreme in Skrewdriver lyrics, Stuart ended up subverting his own intentions. All Stuart's recorded product is camp but it was only with Skrewdriver that he played out his (pre)determined role in the dialectical unfolding of Punk Rock. At the time of his death, Stuart's career was at its peak, he was grossing somewhere between £100 and £200 a week from his 'musical' activities, about the same as the wage for a badly paid labouring job. Not exactly a success story after more than a decade and a half of working towards that elusive *Top Of The Pops* appearance, but typical of both Punk Rock and the financial situations endured by the mentally ill.

IX
SUCK MY LEFT ONE
Riot Grrrl as the penultimate transformation of
Punk Rock

I have already talked about the 'provocative ambiguity' to be found
within the Punk Rock discourse, and it's doubled-edged nature
is only too apparent if one contrasts the number of wimmin musicians to be found in late seventies PUNK ROCK circles with the patriarchal and misogynist attitudes of the 'white power rock and roll'
bands clustered around Skrewdriver. Now, as the PUNK ROCK genre
evolves and is refined over time, many of the wimmin who were
seen as belonging within the entangled PUNK ROCK scenes of the
late seventies have become marginalised or removed to the categories of rock and pop. Where this hasn't been the case, the groups
in which they played tended to be male dominated. For example,
on the West Coast PUNK scene of the late seventies, it seemed virtually obligatory to have a femail bass player but then within pop
and rock discourse, the rhythm section is generally considered to
play a subordinate role to the singer and guitarist(s). It follows
from this that within LA PUNK ROCK groups such as the Germs or
the Alleycats, the femail bass players might have anchored the sound
but they are not thought of as having led these bands.

Thinking of various groups from the late seventies/early eighties who featured, at least for a time, femail members, and who
might once have been considered a part of the new wave explosion, it's incredible to realise how few can still be viewed as falling
within the flexible boundaries of the PUNK ROCK genre. Here's a list
off the top of my head: Cherry Vanilla, Nina Hagen, Passage, Young
Marble Giants, Weekend, Warm, Rubella Ballet, Partisans, Adverts,
Runaways, Poison Girls, Venus And The Razorblades, Zipper, Hagar
The Womb, Patti Smith, Talking Heads, Tom Tom Club, New Or-
der, Slits, Siouxsie And The Banshees, Raincoats, Manicured Noise,
Big In Japan, Mad, X-Ray Spex, Killjoys, Kleenex, Liliput, Mo-
Dettes, ESG, Snatch, Sonic Youth, Prag Vec, Photos, Go Gos,
Cramps, Crass, Au Pairs, B-52s, B-Girls, Delta 5, Human League,
True Life Confessions, Vice Squad, Chaotic Dischord, Selector,
Bodysnatchers, Mood Elevators, Lemon Kittens, Sick Things, Stinky
Toys, Rachel Sweet, Jayne Ayre, Toyah, Hazel O'Conner, Blondie,

Eie Trummerfraun, Trudy, Pulsallama, Teenage Jesus And The Jerks, Rezillos, Revillos, Metrophase, Throbbing Gristle.

I have already stated that I do not wish to use the list as an organising principal and must repeat that many of these bands are not necessarily PUNK ROCK acts. The point I am making is that late seventies PUNK ROCK created a space in which wimmin could play music, even if the evolution of the ideological strand within the genre and its later transformations, as it sought to organise itself around the principles of class and race, served to undercut this initially liberating aspect of the discourse. The 'anyone can do it' attitude of PUNK ROCK, alongside its insistence that making music is not about technical skill, removes one of the major barriers that excludes wimmin from participating in the production of pop records as anything other than a manipulated chanteuse.

Skill, like 'genius', is traditionally a male attribute within our socially constructed notions of gender, and these tend to be counterpoised to what are portrayed as more 'humble' femail qualities such as intuition and empathy. Related to this are notions of the 'skilled' rock musician as an 'artist', an idea that is violently rejected as an oppressive imposition of the dominant culture by those engaged with PUNK ROCK discourse. Since 'artistic creativity' is an area in which traditionally repressed male emotionality is allowed 'legitimate' expression, it is hardly surprising that those propagating patriarchy wish to exclude wimmin from cultural activities serving this function. PUNK ROCK projects itself as 'unartistic', and therefore doesn't automatically erect barriers against the participation of wimmin.

Riot Grrrl was wimmin reasserting themselves within the PUNK ROCK genre and despite the discourse tending towards patriarchal modes of organisation during its class and race based phases, it ultimately tips back into being progressive, which is why nationalist Oi! bands and 'white power rock and roll' groups inevitably abandon this particular cultural form in favour of 'hard' rock. Like the ideological Punk Rock explosion of the late seventies, Riot Grrrl was initially an American phenomenon but the conditions in which it could move from the underground into mass culture only existed in England. The required media infrastructure consisted of a relatively wide range of national newspapers and TV stations, alongside a peculiarly hip and fashion based music and style press. If the years 1976 and 1977 were an amplic period for the PUNK ROCK genre, a time in which a wide variety of musical and fashion currents were entangled and infused, then Oi! and 'white power rock and roll' must be viewed as the cyclical return of the chiselling process, which dominated their evolution despite the necessity for brief amplic periods within each of these subgenres. What had been brought together had to be refined, reduced and reorganised on the basis of class and race. Riot Grrrl, when it was transplanted across the Atlantic and brought into the hot house of British youth culture, should have provided PUNK ROCK with another amplic phase. Unfortunately, this process was completely botched because Huggy Bear, who became the central media icon of the Riot Grrrl movement, initially went along with the press hype and then more or less refused to talk to journalists at the very moment the 'movement' was attaining critical mass. As a consequence, this stage in the dialectical unfolding of ideological Punk Rock went off as a whimper, rather than with the required bang.

In many ways, this section of my text will be very different from the proceeding ones, because I am dealing with a Punk Rock phenomenon that has not, as yet, superseded its amplic phase by acquiring the necessary characteristics to enter a chiselling period. Some readers may have been puzzled as to why I made no mention of bands such as the Business in my section on Oi! To spell it out, although the Business were closely associated with 'street rock' during its amplic phase in the early eighties, musically they are too close to a mainstream rock sound to be considered a part of the evolving Oi! subgenre by someone, such as myself, who is engaged in a very refined chiselling of the ideological Punk Rock discourse. However, my methodological approach to Riot Grrrl will be quite different because its current evolutionary state necessitates an amplic procedure.

Since Huggy Bear were required to take on the role played by the Sex Pistols in an earlier stage of the evolution of the Punk Rock genre, providing a myth around which other bands could organise themselves, it is perfectly feasible to suggest that they were not a Riot Grrrl act. However, since Huggy Bear were unwilling to play out the whole of their allotted role, they failed to rise above their peers and, as a consequence, it is not problematic for me to treat them as an archetypal Riot Grrrl band. Rather than looking at Riot Grrrl music in any detail, I wish to focus on the media coverage the 'movement' generated, because this gives a good indication of what would have happened if Huggy Bear had risen (or if your ideological orientation inclines you towards a less critical perspective, sunk) to a level where they were prepared to fulfil their, at least potentially, 'historic role'. Following a verbal confrontation between Huggy Bear and TV presenter Terry Christian on the 12 February 1993 edition of late nite 'yoof' show *The Word*, the music press cranked up the hype around the band and before long the national media were falling over themselves to cover Riot Grrrl. *Ready, Teddy, Go! Rage Against The Man Machine!* screamed a headline in the New Musical Express on 6 March 1993:

> You've seen Huggy Bear smash up mainstream complacency on *The Word*, you've heard how Bikini Kill take their tops off onstage, you've been baffled by a load of biased ranting on some kind of new punk for women... now prepare yourself for the DEFINITIVE GUIDE TO RIOT GRRRL! This week, Steven Wells goes on the trail of the elusive Huggy Bear, nails them down for a few quotes and power-drills his colours unequivocally to their radical, wonderful mast. Over the page, Liz Evans uncovers the thrilling, subversive history of the American Riot Grrrl movement, and checks the opinions of role model Kim Gordon, plus Miki Berenyi and Emma Anderson of Lush, and Come's Thalia Zedek. Next week, Bikini Kill reveal themselves exclusively to NME and riot grrran Lydia Lunch lashes out at the whole scene. Take cover, cynics... and remember kids – Boy! Girl! Revolution Now!

If this sounds like a manipulative bit of hype to you, then, like me, you're never going to be sixteen again. While *Melody Maker* was quicker off the mark in pumping up the phenomena (this particular publication had an advantage over its chief rival because two members of Huggy Bear shared a house with one of its staff journalists), the NME's larger circulation caused the mainstream media to take its pronouncements as definitive. Several music journalists were unashamedly hyping Riot Grrrl and this was just what the 'movement' (which didn't as yet exist in the UK) required if its amplic phase was to be productive. I saw for myself how effective this strategy was because for several years I'd allowed Erica Smith, who produces the feminist comics journal *GirlFrenzy*, to use my post box address. After *GirlFrenzy* appeared in the list of essential Riot Grrrl reading run by the NME, mail poured in despite the fact that Smith did not consider herself to be a Riot Grrrl and had never heard of the phenomena before the media hype began.

The number of letters *GirlFrenzy* received soared, without much of this extra mail bearing any relationship to the content of the magazine. There were numerous enquiries about Riot Grrrl from journalists and disc jockeys, which were all thrown straight in the bin. However, replies with relevant addresses were sent to the numerous teenage grrrls, most studying at provincial colleges, who wanted to get involved in Riot Grrrl. Almost without exception, these would state that the letter writer knew the NME sucked as badly as the rest of the media, but that since they didn't know any Riot Grrrls and were desperate to get in touch with some, this was their only source of information. Since the NME piece was taken as authoritative by the national media, several daily newspapers cited *GirlFrenzy* as a leading Riot Grrrl publication, and the *Independent On Sunday* of 14 March 1993 even reproduced the front cover of the magazine in its feature on the phenomena. Under the headline *Rock Against Men Is Music To The Riot Grrrls' Ears*, Hester Matthewman reported that a 'new movement of radical young feminists draws its inspiration from man-hating, all-women bands'. Matthewman provided the information you'd expect:

> Riot Grrrls are here. And they're angrrry. Described by the rock-music press as girl-punk revolutionaries, these radical young feminists are not keen on men. ('Man-hating is simply the attitude that most men suck, and they do,' according to Jo of the band Huggy Bear.) Riot Grrrl bands have been grabbing media attention recently – Huggy Bear attacked Terry Christian, presenter of Channel 4's *The Word*, on the air, and fans had to be ejected from the studio.

Ten days later, under the headline *Angry Young Women*, Caroline Sullivan was reporting pretty much the same thing in the *Guardian*:

> Riot Grrrls UK are following punk's initial trajectory. There are fanzines, embryonic grrrl gangs and at the hub, Huggy Bear. The London and Brighton based quintet have already had their Bill Grundy Moment, *a la* the Sex Pistols. Last month, they were ejected from *The Word* after noisily accusing presenter Terry Christian of sexism. *The Word* reportedly demanded an apology... But while the Pistols were aimless, even nihilistic, Huggy Bear are focused and 'girl-positive'. Their aim is Girl Power and they particularly detest boy rock...

Save The World? Not A Hope Grrrls Anne Barrowclough raged in the *Daily Mail* of 27 March 1993:

They screech, they spit, they snarl, they swear. Every word they scream through the microphone is a prayer against men. When their music stops, you are left with a pounding head, buzzing ear drums and no doubt that Men are The Enemy. Meet the Riot Grrrls, the latest, nastiest phenomenon to enter the British music scene... Riot Grrrls don't like men much. They don't like anything much, except other women – as long as they're 'enlightened' and don't 'act like their parents'... Riot Grrrls are to music what Damien Hirst is to art. They're angry, anarchistic, full of loathing. They call themselves feminists but theirs is a feminism of rage and, even, fear. At its simplest, their message is that men have held women back in the music industry and subjected them to violence in everyday life. By forming all-girl bands and screaming tunelessly at their audiences, they believe they can change the balance and ensure that women rule OK. What makes them frightening is the virulence of their message. They attempt to instil in young fans a deep loathing of men, based on the fear of violence that most young women have. Their (male) detractors have dubbed them, with reason, 'feminazis'... In many ways their actions contradict what they are trying to achieve. Bikini Kill have an especially revolting *modus operandi* in which they take off their tops, dance in their bras, and even toss sanitary towels into the audience... Not only do they show off their bodies on stage – some claiming proudly to be strippers – but they depend on men as their backing bands and technicians. At the gigs, however, the fans remain convinced these girls are going to change the world...

The coverage spluttered on through the summer, with, for ex-ample, the *Daily Star* of 9 July 1993 carrying the report *I Brave The Riot Girls* by John Poole:

They are the toughest, meanest group of feminists since women began burning their bras back in the swinging Sixties. The so-called Riot Girls play rough 'n' ready rock music and they list MAN-HATING among their favourite hobbies. Shabbily-dressed bands such as Huggy Bear, Bikini Kill, Lunachicks, Bratmobile and L7 are ruthlessly ruled by outrageous guru Courtney Love. It was her hardcore punk band Hole, which gave birth to an army of angry girls who wanted to take over 'boring' male rock 'n' roll... And so a scorching Saturday evening finds me outside the Dome, a premier London rock venue... To steady my nerves, I have an ice-cold beer in the bar next door... A gang of teenage girl bruisers has followed me into the pub. A shiver goes down my spine as an incredibly scruffy girl spits: 'Oh No! It's the Daily Star!'... I scurry away in a cab. The chilling screams are ringing in my ears and I'm just thankful I wasn't stripped naked and hung from the nearest lamp-post...

Daisy Waugh in the *Evening Standard* of 16 August 1993 was less revealing about her sexual fears and frustrations and her piece, carried under the headline *Don't Mess With The Girls Who Just Wanna Be Grrrls*, was mildly sympathetic towards Riot Grrrl:

> Riot Grrrls are angry. Imagine a collection of 15 year-olds who have recently discovered feminism – and rock – and what a wicked, unfair world is out there. Imagine that sort of righteous, adolescent anger, these are girls who like to say f***, who like the space to be allowed a bit of (admittedly half-baked) self-expression, who believe in anarchy and revolution. Their ideas may be babyish. But at least they *have* some. At least they've learned there's more to life than simpering over the contents of their dressing tables... Lucky girls, I wish there'd been a gang of them back home in Taunton when I was very young.

If much of the press coverage was silly and inaccurate, that hardly matters; its function should have been to create a buzz, excitement, a scene. The dilemma faced by Riot Grrrl once Huggy Bear pulled out of the hype wasn't that its media reportage was distorted, the problem was that there wasn't enough of it and what there was simply wasn't sensational enough. Riot Grrrl, in as far as it has ever really existed, was created by the press, which threw together various disparate phenomenon and labelled this jumble a movement. People don't necessarily believe everything they read in the papers and the success of publications such as the *Weekly World News* and the *Sunday Sport* is partly based on the fact that their readers enjoy testing both their scepticism and their gullibility.

Without doubt, 'Riot Grrrls' and potential 'Riot Grrrls' were the most gullible consumers of media reports on the phenomena, necessarily so, because in this way they were able to realise their productive role in the 'creation of culture'. It was essential for several thousand teenage grrrls to believe this movement really existed, so that it could become a material reality. Unfortunately, the young wimmin who became Riot Grrrls after reading media hype about the phenomenon, or in some cases upon seeing themselves cited as the leaders of the 'movement', were greatly handicapped by the fact that it was almost universally stated that they refused to talk to the press. This 'misrepresentation' was widely believed in Riot Grrrl circles, although it was patently untrue, and resulted in the instant 'movement' failing to make proper use of the vehicle the initial music press hype had created for it. The extraordinary success of late seventies PUNK ROCK was grounded in the fact that most of those who became embroiled in the media discourse around which their activities had been organised were only too happy to go along with any hype whatsoever.

While a theatrical critique of the media is common enough in PUNK ROCK, Riot Grrrl's tragedy was that its devotees mistook the rhetoric attributed to them by the press for reality. In doing so, they pushed the absurdly simplistic critique of the media found in much late seventies PUNK ROCK to its logical conclusion. To focus on just one example, the theme runs through many of the lyrics to be found on *TV Tube Heart*, the first Radiators From Space album (Chiswick Records, London 1977). The rhetorical nature of the PUNK ROCK critique of the media is readily evident from *Television Screen*, the Radiators first single and the opening track on their long player. The singer rants 'I'm gonna sock my Telecaster through the television screen,' and that he's 'never seen more than a tenner a week.' Now it's quite obvious that if the second statement is true, he would not have been able to afford an expensive guitar, Telecasters are great instruments but, unfortunately, they don't come cheap. Of course, it's possible the singer stole the guitar, but then if he's adept at ripping off expensive musical equipment, crime should have provided him with more than 'a tenner a week'. Other media fixated songs on the record include *Enemies*, which responds to press coverage of a murder at one of the band's gigs; *Prison Bars* a rant about how the lines, or 'bars', that make up a television picture result in everybody looking seven inches high; *Press Gang* with its chant of 'media poison in my bloodstream'; and *Sunday World*, the title of a newspaper lying on the floor in the front cover photo of the band watching TV. The back cover of the album features a photograph of the group standing around a smashed television, an image that works precisely because it is a cliché.

With these issues in mind, it ought to be obvious why I have focused my attention on the 'mainstream' media, rather than 'underground' fanzines, which are considered to be of major importance to the PUNK ROCK phenomenon by 'commentators' such as Tricia Henry. It should be equally apparent that I am chiefly interested in treating PUNK ROCK in its various forms as an evolving musical genre. Fanzines are really a second order activity, most of them wouldn't exist if there was no PUNK ROCK music to write about.

While someone wishing to deal with PUNK ROCK as a 'subculture' may find the content of fanzines 'illuminating', I am not a social historian and have no interest in this type of 'archaeology'. In the course of preparing this text, I did look through a pile of old fanzines, things like *Sniffin' Glue* and *Ripped & Torn*, as well as the book *Punk* edited by Julie Davis (Millington, London 1977) which consists of bits and bobs about bands written by 'zine editors. I originally read much of this stuff when I was fourteen or fifteen and at the time considered it 'crucial', now it appears utterly tedious, inaccurate and uninformative. In looking for information about individual bands, the mainstream music press was much more useful, which isn't to say that 'zines don't have a useful function in opening up possibilities for the individuals who produce them, thereby leading them on to better and more interesting things. However, as a vehicle for either 'creativity' or 'communication' they are, by and large, an embarrassment.

No doubt, many of the Riot Grrrl bands consider fanzines to be an important feature of their scene, certainly Huggy Bear and Bikini Kill had a propensity for handing out xeroxed manifestos at their own gigs. Likewise, concerts are seen by many fans as an opportunity to peddle their hastily assembled collages and scribbled texts in xerox form. The booklet accompanying a Bikini Kill CD entitled *The First Two Records* (Kill Rock Stars, Olympia 1994), contains this among its copious sleeve notes:

> To force some forever identity on other people is stupid. Point out inconsistencies in their behaviour, explain how they are not 'truly what they say' because you saw them 'do this' one time... why? Because it is easier to deal with cardboard cut outs than real people, cuz a lot of us pretend like we're the center of the universe sometimes and everyone is just background extras to the movie we imagine we star in. WELL WHILE WE ARE ALL ARGUING ABOUT WHOSE GONNA GET TO OPEN FOR THE MELVINS, WHOSE GONNA WEAR WHAT TO THE PARTY, WHO IS LAME / TAME BECAUSE THEY PERPETUATE THIS THING WE HATE, WHO IS NOT REALLY A PUNK ROCKER CUZ 'I remember when he / she used to listen to Duran Duran', THE REVOLUTION IS GOING DOWN... no it's not happening without us, it is just plain not happening at all... it is going down to the gurgling sound of our own voices, reproducing the voices of our parents in a slightly altered way, the TV people... trying to dictate to each other what is and what isn't cool or revolutionary or true resistance, what is or isn't true in other people's

lives... In order for me to exist I must believe that two contradictory things can exist in the same space. This is not a choice I make, it just is...

And so the torch of oedipal rebellion is passed down to another generation, and there is a distinction that needs to be made here between our subcultural and our genetic 'parents'. It remains a cliché to state that we should not base our understanding of other people's activities solely on the claims they make about the meaning of their actions. As was the case with Oi! it was precisely because Riot Grrrl did not exist that the music press felt compelled to invent it. It is therefore hardly surprising that within Riot Grrrl we find traces of ideological Punk Rock's previous stages of development. The notions of class war, race war and sex war are interlinked, and despite their theatrical presentation within the Punk Rock discourse, the national press was keen to stress that hate and violence was a major component in each of the concepts that marked the genre's successive stages of development.

While neither the London based Voodoo Queens with their Anglo-Indian line-up, nor the Japanese band Shonen Knife, may actually consider themselves to be Riot Grrrls, it is perfectly feasible for me to treat them as being subsumed within this category because the subgenre has yet to supersede its amplic phase. Thus one is able to report Riot Grrrl as presenting the issue of racial identity and difference, raised negatively in the previous stage of the ongoing unfolding of the ideological Punk Rock subgenre, as a positive resolution of this issue. The meeting of different cultural traditions under the integrating rubric of the evolving and pata-national PUNK ROCK musical discourse can be cited as a fine example of the incontestable fact that 'miscegenation is the creative principle at work in evolution'. While the individuals who belong to the various Riot Grrrl bands come from a diverse range of backgrounds, it should not surprise anybody that the bass player with Mambo Taxi had previously been in the Belgian Oi! group Comrade. And just as the entangled late seventies PUNK ROCK phenomena had an elliptical relationship with 'exploitation' band the Runaways, it now appears inevitable that a group like Shampoo would emerge on the pop scene at the same time as Riot Grrrl.

It seems unlikely that Riot Grrrl will ever attain the critical mass necessary to have much of an impact on mainstream culture. This failure will in its turn slow down the evolutionary unfolding of ideological Punk Rock. Nevertheless, over an indeterminate period, Riot Grrrl must transform quantity into quality, the emphasis on youth, evident in the word Grrrl, giving way to a more general concern with femininity, and this must ultimately resolve itself into anxiety about Gaia, or Mother Earth. This explains why the New Wave Of New Wave hype recently whipped up by the music press failed to ignite. Just as 'you can never step into the same river twice' (due to the ongoing flow of water, any given river is constantly changing), it is equally impossible to repeat any stage of ideological Punk Rock once it has unfolded, or, indeed, for the subgenre to deviate from the course of development I have outlined. I do not wish to pass judgement on the musical merits of the various bands associated with NWONW, I need merely observe that despite absurd claims to the contrary they have nothing to do with Punk Rock because the only principle around which it is now possible to organise a fresh development of this subgenre is that of ecology.

An extraordinarily premature attempt to organise music in this fashion can be found on Vegan Reich's *Hardline* EP (Hardline, California, no date but early nineties), which unfortunately adopts the non-PUNK ROCK format of hardcore. A leaflet accompanying the record states:

> The time has come for an ideology and for a movement, that is both physically and morally strong enough, to do battle against the forces of evil that are destroying the earth (and all life upon it). One that cannot be bought, nor led astray by temptation. A movement free of the vices that sedate the mind and weaken the body. An ideology that is pure and righteous, without contradictions or inconsistencies. One that judges all things by one standard and emphasizes personal responsibility and accountability above all else. An overall view on life that not only deals with the external, but also the internal – realizing that a physical entity of oppression, such as the capitalist system (where all life is deemed an expendable resource), is merely an outward manifestation of the warped values held by the people who run the institutions that control our lives, influence our culture and destroy the earth...

Vegan Reich's song lyrics are as much fun as their idealist literature, and only the music lets the record down. *I, The Jury* is typical of the four tracks on the EP:

I'm thru with tolerance / No more acceptance of your crimes / I don't care about your freedom coz your action restricts mine / And the rights of those you step on everyday / As you drag down all in your way as you slowly self-decay / Smoking a cash crop / I don't care if you die / But the animals tested / Should they pay that price? / Or those who are near you who have got no choice but to breath secondhand smoke you create / And what of those who are killed or maimed as you drink and drive as if it's a game? / Or the third world peasants forced to make your cocaine / Enslaved and impoverished for the choices you've made / To feed your weakness another vice / To satisfy your hunger / You never think twice of the pain it causes others / You just talk about your rights / As you eat the flesh from another that you denied life / Freedom is not just a one way street / You've got no right to choose when it gets in the way / Of others well being, their rights, their needs / To live in peace in a sane society / And everything you do does get in the way of all that surrounds you / So don't ever say that it harms only you and it's your choice to make / Coz a weak link in the chain will break the whole thing / And that I cannot tolerate / Won't let you pull us all down the drain / I'm thru with looking the other way / It's fucking time to set things straight / For too long you've been the one to dictate the way the rest of us live / And that's now gonna change if you wish to remain / Then stay in your place coz you fuck us up again / And I won't hesitate to infringe your rights / To take them away / to be the judge and jury and make you fucking pay for the crimes you commit day after day / Coz only with you stopped will our lives be truly free!

Vegan Reich have mastered the empty rhetoric of PUNK ROCK but not the genre's musical sound. However, their words are a foretaste of what the future undoubtedly holds. Thus we are able to grasp all four stages in the dialectical unfolding of ideological Punk Rock. The vague radicalism of groups such as the Fugs and the MC5 was transformed in England during the late seventies into a concern with class which only found its full realisation in Oi!. Increasing the level of pseudo-intransigence, which is a natural tendency among those participating in this discourse, led to rhetoric about the 'proletariat' being more narrowly defined in terms of the 'white working class'. The racism of the 'white power rock and roll' bands was predicated on notions about the 'healthy' masculinity of 'white working class' youth. As the theatrical potential of this 'masculinity' was quantitatively increased, it was reduced to the level of a caricature, and was thereby inverted, becoming camp and ultimately resulting in 'top faces' on the 'white power rock and roll' scene, such as Nicky Crane, admitting (at least to each other) that they were gay. In this way, through the bridging concept of sexuality, the Punk Rock dialectic shifts its mode of organisation from theatrics about race to rhetoric about gender, with the resulting emergence of the Riot Grrrl 'movement'. As I have just pointed out, within the Punk Rock genre a quantitative increase in levels of concern about femininity will result in the discourse ultimately adopting Mother Earth, or ecology, as its ideological organising principle.

I have already stated that within this particular dialectic the cosmic counterpart of class is Earth, while the mythical equivalent of race is Water, with gender being represented by Air. It necessarily follows that ecology corresponds to Fire. The same elements can be seen dialectically unfolding in the development of mass political ideologies during the course of the past century – the modern workers' movement arose in the epoch preceding the First World War; the interwar period was an era of fascist triumph, in which bestial racial theories gained ground; feminism made a huge impact on the lives of ordinary men and wimmin in the post-war period, with feminist theory reaching a new maturity in the nineteen-seventies; while a world-wide ecological movement developed in the nineteen-eighties. I have no desire to offer an explanation for these correspondences, I simply wish to point them out.

X
CONCLUDING UNACADEMIC
POSTSCRIPT
A literary conceit

Until the publishing industry began spewing out books that were supposed to be about PUNK ROCK but which, without exception, failed to define their subject, I had no interest in providing an account of this particular form of genre music. It seems extraordinary that I am unable to find evidence of anyone lifting ideas about 'genre' from film theory and applying them to PUNK ROCK. As I have already pointed out, this inability to deal with the subject sensibly, or indeed, despite the fact that much of the material is humorous, with any wit, is a common failure among both 'popular' and 'academic' accounts of PUNK ROCK.

I consider the composition of lengthy books about PUNK ROCK an absurd pursuit; the subject simply doesn't warrant this kind of labour. However, while it would be gratifying if the present text could act as a coda to 'debate' on the issue, it is unlikely that I have produced anything more than a prolegomenon to any future discussion of PUNK ROCK. If this short work prevents one writer from repeating the ludicrous claims made by George Gimarc in his lousy *Punk Diary: 1970 – 1979* (St. Martin's Press, New York 1994), then it will have served some purpose. Gimarc writes that what makes his book 'unlike any other rock book is that it treats the scene on a day to day basis, diary style, the way it actually happened. The only way that this tangled web can make sense.'

In fact, there are many ways in which people make 'sense' of PUNK ROCK, and the present text is merely the best theoretical account of the phenomenon to date. No doubt, various clowns will attempt to dismiss the dialectic whose existence I have sketched as absurd, while in 'reality' I have done no more or less than any scientist, that is to say I've looked for a pattern amongst a particular set of phenomena and found one. I have not tinkered with the facts to make them fit my theory, the theory fits the facts and until someone like me, who possesses a modicum of intelligence, wastes a couple of weeks pursuing similar trivialities, my text will remain the only work on PUNK ROCK that is worth reading.

Since I was already immersed in the PUNK ROCK discourse and the present work merely required that I (re)orientate myself within the tradition, I was aware long before I began to compose the preceding paragraphs that it would be a mistake to approach the subject with reverence. Likewise, since I do not wish the present text to be treated as a work of reference, it would be counterproductive to include a discography, bibliography or index. I am well aware that such a stand will have an adverse effect upon the sales of this text to libraries and academic institutions, but I have already made it clear that PUNK ROCK is an evolving musical genre, with flexible parameters, and these insights would be undercut if I made compromises of this type. Besides, I deliberately operate outside the confines of the college system and therefore have no need of formal academic trappings to secure either a tenure or a promotion.

While I still derive pleasure from listening to PUNK ROCK records, I would not want to be teenage again. It's been a very long time indeed since I last felt any desire to spend every other night in a dank, crowded club watching an endless succession of no-hope bands strut their stuff. However, manic gig attendance does have its uses; if nothing else, going to PUNK ROCK concerts taught me the (psycho)geography of Greater London. And even as a fourteen year old I was smart enough to realise that PUNK ROCK wasn't profound. We change and yet remain the same. While cretins look for the meaning of life in plastic platters and morons seek it in tomes by Kierkegaard and Kant, 'intelligence' is active and knows that the culture we've inherited is something to be manipulated rather than passively consumed. Let the dead bury their dead, we will blaze a trail to new modes of being...

Stewart Home
London
December 1994

APPENDIX
A COSMETIC UNDERGROUND
Lipstick Traces: a secret history of the
twentieth century by Greil Marcus
(Harvard University Press $29.95)

Now that the prospect of economic unification within the European Community has become a rapidly approaching reality, many of the conglomerate's leading figures feel that the nations they control are going to achieve a position of dominance within the world. As a consequence, a number of previously obscure European cultural movements are being promoted in an attempt to challenge America's position of hegemony within the arts. Working backwards from PUNK ROCK, journalist Greil Marcus has set out to historify two of these rehabilitated groups by situating them in the context of a tradition which he traces back through Dada to the beliefs of twelfth-century Christian heretics. Since Marcus is chiefly concerned with the recent past, he begins by telling us that:

> This book is about a single, serpentine fact: late in 1976 a record called *Anarchy In The UK* was issued in London, and this event launched a transformation of pop music all over the world. Made by a four-man rock 'n' roll band called the Sex Pistols, and written by singer Johnny Rotten, the song distilled, in crudely poetic form, a critique of modern society once set out by a small group of Paris-based intellectuals.

The group of Paris-based intellectuals to whom Marcus refers were the Lettriste International, who he claims were 'refounded in 1957 at a conference of European avant-garde artists as the Situationist International.'

A very crude form of reductionism is at work here, since to suggest that the Sex Pistols simply took up a critique elaborated by earlier avant-garde groups is to ignore historical, geographical and class difference. Likewise, the Situationist International (SI) was far more than a simple refounding of the Lettriste International (LI); it brought together a number of individuals who'd been involved with splinter groups from revolutionary Surrealism and who wished to re-launch the Surrealist project on a new footing. Particularly significant among the latter were Asger Jorn and Constant who'd previously held membership of the COBRA movement. While the LI had been a tiny Parisian grouplet, the SI (although few in number) counted among its members Algerian, Belgian, British, Danish, Dutch, French and Italian nationals. As a result, both the theory and practice of the SI were broader (and less coherent) than that of the LI. Thus while the LI emphasised the necessity of living the cultural revolution, the SI – in its early years – produced works of art in far greater quantity (and many would say of a far higher quality) than the only group Marcus acknowledges as its precursor.

To return to the Sex Pistols, *Anarchy In The UK* was not written by Johnny Rotten but by all four members of the band. This is one of many trivial misrepresentations which illustrate the author's refusal to come to terms with collective or collaborative projects. He reduces the Sex Pistols to their singer and the post-war avant-garde to a single member of the Situationist International, Guy Debord; two celebrities whose fame depersonalises them to such a degree that they've become representations of individuality rather than autonomous subjects consciously striking out in a direction of their own choice.

By transforming Rotten and Debord into figureheads of PUNK and Situationism, by treating them as archetypes, Marcus simultaneously cancels out any sense of the specificity of the movements to which they belonged. Rather than seeing PUNK as a reaction on the part of a specific sub-strata of English society to rapid inflation, the growth of mass unemployment, the musical tastes of the preceding generation and the general sense of cultural devastation which ravaged Britain in the mid-seventies, Marcus treats it as little more than fall-out from left-bank bohemianism. He has no sense of the fundamental difference between a trend within popular culture and the ideological beliefs of a tiny clique of intellectuals, such as the Situationists, whose journals reached a peak circulation of a few thousand copies.

Another element missing from *Lipstick Traces* is an active engagement with politics; Marcus makes several rhetorical denunciations of capitalism but since these don't contain even a hint of a class based perspective, they are as abstract as his misunderstanding of PUNK. Anyone who can suggest that PUNK 'was,

finally, no more than an art statement,' doesn't understand (or is deliberately mystifying) the class basis of culture. As a current within popular culture, PUNK tended to be consumed as a series of narratives with which its audience could identify; central among these were stories of conflict between the dispossessed and those in authority (cf. *Anarchy In The UK, God Save The Queen* and *White Riot*). As a discourse PUNK subordinated form to content, whereas Situationist theory which emphasises aesthetic distancing (most obviously in the concept of 'the Spectacle') – albeit as a disagreeable phenomena – reflects the concerns of bourgeois culture. Members of the PUNK community rarely considered the means by which they communicated (or the way in which they apprehended the world) to be problematic, whereas for the Situationists 'everything that was directly lived has moved away into representation' (Thesis 1 of Debord's *Society Of The Spectacle*). Thus in the Situationist critique, as in any bourgeois ideology, there is a tendency to liquidate meaningful content by subordinating it to form and formal innovation. The Situationist assertion that the entire world is dominated by an essentially banal set of social and economic relations represents a particularly extreme version of this trend and wilfully glosses over the differences between east and west, first and third world, popular and high culture – thereby discouraging resistance to localised oppression by clothing Power with a monolithic appearance.

Linked to the issues of class and taste is the process of historification. Marcus wants to elevate PUNK to the status of art and bring the Lettriste and Situationist movements into the accepted canon of art history. The question as to how and why this process of canonisation takes place is never directly addressed by Marcus, although it seems reasonable to assume he's reflected upon the issue – since *Lipstick Traces* is simply one among many recent publications which have played a role in celebrating the work and personality of Guy Debord. The tendency in much of the secondary literature on the SI to view Debord as 'a genius' shifts attention away from the issues addressed by the Situationists and onto Debord's personal achievement in allegedly confronting capitalism.

The emphasis Marcus places upon personalities ultimately nullifies any sense of individuality which his subjects might possess. The links drawn between free spirit heretics and members of the Lettriste, Situationist and PUNK movements, are forged without acknowledgement of the fact that the former lived in feudal communities while the latter were attempting to effect change within industrialised societies. Since the mental sets and social networks of individuals living under capitalism are fundamentally different to those shared by members of a feudal community, comparisons between the two are specious.

The device used to link these diverse individuals and movements is the metaphor of the medium; Johnny Rotten is a passive creator whose body is taken over by what Marcus describes as 'the voice,' but which we might just as well call the muse, or God – because it's a higher authority. In his description of the last Sex Pistols concert, Marcus portrays Johnny Rotten as a puppet whose actions are controlled by an occult force:

> As in other moments on the same stage on the same night, as in so many moments on the singles the Sex Pistols put out over the previous year, he seemed not to know what he was saying. He seemed not to be himself, whoever that was, once more he was less singing a song than being sung by it.

With the concept of 'the voice,' a hidden authority which (dis)organises the world, Marcus abandons any need for a rational explanation of the events he describes. Such a mode of discourse has more in common with the simple faith of a priest, than the considered reflections of a critic or historian; it is a creed which, with its refusal of difference, does a gross disservice both to the post-war avant-garde and the PUNK music Marcus claims to love.

Originally published in *New Art Examiner* March 1990, i.e. nine months after it was commissioned and written.

The Voidoid
Richard Hell

"The Voidoid was written in 1973 in a little furnished room on East 10th Street. I was staying with Jennifer ("my thoughts and me are like ships that pass in the night") in her apartment down the block overlooking the graveyard at St. Mark's Church. Every day I'd take a cheap bottle of wine with me across the street to the $16-a-week room I'd rented for writing. The method was I'd keep going till I got to the end of a single-spaced page, which was pretty far. I'd wake up an hour later and have to drink. A lot of water. Sometimes afterwards if I had some extra money I'd go to the pharmacy on Second Avenue and buy a bottle of codeine cough syrup and come back and lie on the cot again. The Neon Boys were stalled because we couldn't find a second guitar player...

I still like this book a lot. It's smirched up with *Maldoror*, but I relished that and flaunted it because Lautréamont was my brother. In fact when I typed up the final draft, I imitated the format of the New Directions edition of his book and jammed the text in thick dark blocks inside big wide margins. I wanted to lay it all bare and expose it there; the paper sheets like settings for something, weird jewels, filthy aerial night photos, which when you looked inside them came alive. That's what I wanted. I hope it does something for you. I still can't help wishing it could do something intense."

Fiction A5 96 pages
1899598022 Paperback £5.95

My Fault
Billy Childish

Born into the emerging middle classes of the 1950s, Billy Childish takes us on a nightmarish voyage through a blighted childhood which culminates in his being sexually abused by a friend of the family. Stumbling onward into adolescence he exposes his desperate attempts to make sense of a world distorted by alcohol, bullies and yes-men.

This striking first novel, or "creative confession", is at turns hilarious and harrowing. Laced with lines of unforgettable poetry, it is that rare and wonderful thing – a book which had to be written.

A legendary figure in underground writing, painting and music, Billy Childish was born in Chatham, England in 1959. After completing secondary education at 16 he entered the naval dockyard at Chatham as an apprentice stonemason. Unable to settle in work, there followed an unsatisfactory spell at art school and thirteen years of unemployment.

Fiction A5 366 pages
1899598065 Paperback £7.95

Flickers of the Dreamachine
edited by Paul Cecil

As more and more people immerse themselves in cyberspace, and Virtual Reality freaks claim to have discovered the inner being, it is timely to recall the pioneering art and science of the Dreamachine. Devised in the early '60s by artist Brion Gysin and mathematician Ian Sommerville, the Dreamachine is still the simplest and most effective of all brain wave stimulators. It is the first object specifically designed to be seen through closed eyes.

Notable Dreamachine users include William Burroughs, Derek Jarman and (allegedly) Kurt Cobain. Based on the principle that flickering light triggers brain wave responses, the Dreamachine's impact is startling: images emerge from the dark and dreams become tangible. *Flickers* is the story of this amazing invention, a voyage into the art and magic of inner space.

This book includes full construction plans, seminal essays by Gysin and Sommerville, as well as extensive extracts from W. Grey Walter's The Living Brain, which provided the neurological theory for the first machines. Alongside these technical writings are essays by some of the artists who have worked with the Dreamachine, including Genesis P-Orridge, Terry Wilson, Ira Cohen and many others. *Flickers of the Dreamachine* is edited by Paul Cecil, the co-founder of Temple Press and an acknowledged expert on esoteric philosophy.

Non-Fiction 210x210mm 132 pages
1899598030 Paperback £7.95

Too Drugfucked for Print?

Our range of finest quality spoken-word compact discs may provide the answer

Hexentexts
A Creation Books Sampler

CODE1 / 1899598510 62:47 £9.95

Over an hour of (sometimes simultaneous) words and music from the cutting edge of Creation's list: James Havoc with Rob Young from Primal Scream; Geraldine Monk and her lovable brogue; Alan Moore wakes his Snakes; Mick Norman chews the fat with Stewart Home; Jeremy Reed tells us about his androgynous worldview; plus the inimitable Aaron Williamson.

Kathy Acker – **Pussy**

CODE2 / 1899598529 60:25 £9.95

During a speaking tour of England in Autumn 1994 CodeX invited Ms. Acker to record sections of work in progress, which were then reassembled into a new and exclusive work. Anyone familiar with this author's unforgettable live performances will not need to be told of the extra dimension her voice brings to her texts.

Richard Hell – **Go Now**

CODE3 / 1899598537 21:37 £6.95

This recording is taken from the first two chapters of a brand new work published by Fourth Estate and features guitar accompaniment by ex-Voidoid Robert Quine.

Iain Banks & Gary Lloyd – **The Bridge**

CODE4 / 1899598547 21:37 £9.95

A stunning audio re-working of the 1984 novel featuring a musical soundtrack composed by Gary Lloyd and performed by a cast of 45 musicians. Narrative performance by Banks himself.

To order any of the preceding items send a cheque, postal order or IMO (payable to CodeX, in Sterling, drawn on a British bank) to Dept. C, P.O. Box 148, Hove, East Sussex, BN3 3DQ. Prices include postage worldwide and are correct at the time of printing.